P9-DDX-273

Leading Your Ministry

Developing the Mind of a Priest and the Soul of a Prophet

LEADERSHIP *LIS* INSIGHT SERIES
LEADERSHIP *LIS* INSIGHT SERIES
LEADERSHIP *LIS* INSIGHT SERIES

Leading Your Ministry

HERB MILLER, EDITOR

A moment of insight is worth a lifetime of experience

ALAN E. NELSON

Abingdon Press
Nashville

LEADING YOUR MINISTRY

Copyright © 1996 by Abingdon Press

All rights reserved.
No part of this work may be reproduced or transmitted in any form or by any means, electronic or mechanical, including photocopying and recording, or by any information storage or retrieval system, except as may be expressly permitted by the 1976 Copyright Act or in writing from the publisher. Requests for permission should be addressed in writing to Abingdon Press, P.O. Box 801, 201 Eighth Avenue South, Nashville, TN 37202.

This book is printed on recycled, acid-free paper.

Library of Congress Cataloging-in-Publication Data

Nelson, Alan E.
    Leading your ministry: developing the mind of a priest and the
soul of a prophet/Alan E. Nelson; Herb Miller, editor.
        p.   cm.—(Leadership insights series)
    Includes bibliographical references.
    ISBN 0-687-01964-8 (alk. paper)
    1. Clergy —Office.   2. Christian leadership.   3. Pastoral
theology.   I. Miller, Herb.   II. Title.   III. Series.
BV660.2.N37   1996
253—dc20   96-12804
                                                                    CIP

Unless otherwise noted, Scripture quotations are from the HOLY BIBLE, NEW INTERNATIONAL VERSION®. Copyright © 1973, 1978, 1984 by the International Bible Society. Used by permission of Zondervan Bible Publishers. All rights reserved.

Scripture quotations noted KJV are from the King James Version of the Bible.

96 97 98 99 00 01 02 03 04 05 — 10 9 8 7 6 5 4 3 2 1

MANUFACTURED IN THE UNITED STATES OF AMERICA

957

91128

To my Christian parents,
Everett and June Nelson,
who have supported me in my adventures
since childhood

Thanks also to
Dr. Joseph Rost and
the University of San Diego
leadership faculty who broadened my ability
to understand and study leadership

CONTENTS

Contents

FOREWORD

A cartoon character is busily winding up his kite string. He explains to a little girl bystander the scientific details of why kites fly—how the ratio of weight to surface area is known as "sail loading," and so forth. The little girl listens to his lengthy technical explanation about kites and praises his knowledge. In the concluding picture she asks him why his kite is down the sewer.

Despite the countless books and articles on the art/science of leadership published in recent years, pastors recognize that something is still missing. Reading and applying this literature does not always keep our kites in the air. Alan Nelson addresses this missing link in contemporary leadership education. Moving beyond what leaders *do* to what leaders *are*, Nelson helps us to see that knowing the mechanics of leadership is not enough.

Effective pastors are change agents, which means that they must know (1) what to change, (2) why it must be changed, and (3) how to bring to bear the resources that can accomplish the needed change. Leaders must point their knowledge toward the right goals.

A railroad conductor started collecting tickets. The first passenger had a ticket for the wrong city. The conductor explained to the distraught passenger that she would have to change trains at the next station. To the conductor's amazement, the next three passengers also had the wrong tickets. Suddenly, the painful truth dawned: The conductor was on the wrong train!

Effective leaders must give up the illusion that they will do everything right. They must, however, do the right things. Effective leaders must be on the right train. If they are not, working harder and harder at the old leadership models leaves them more and more frustrated. Nelson helps pastors to examine their leadership paradigms as well as their leadership traits to make sure they move toward goals that make sense in this period of church history.

In 1771, John Wesley assigned Francis Asbury the task of evangelizing the American frontier. Asbury's leadership methods were often called "authoritarian" and he had many critics. Asbury did not do everything right, but he knew the right things to do. For the next thirty-two years Asbury crossed the Allegheny mountains sixty-two times in order to be present among the hundreds of young circuit riders he recruited for frontier ministry. He rode 270,000 miles and wore out five horses. The results: By 1784, more than 14,000 Methodists related to forty-two American circuits. By 1844, long after Asbury's death in 1816, the momentum was still building. One million Methodists in 3,988 circuits were led by 7,730 local preachers!

Asbury succeeded not because he had all the traits of an effective leader but because he picked the right goals and the right leadership paradigm. He got on the right train. Nelson helps pastors to see into the what and the how of those leadership essentials for contemporary church leaders.

—Herb Miller, Lubbock, Texas

INTRODUCTION

THE BURNING BUSH

The bush burned. Its radiant glow and dancing flames caught the attention of the renegade Egyptian, the converted shepherd. The call of Moses was unique. How many of God's leaders can testify to being ordained in such a manner? Although nothing had changed for generations, it was time to release the brick baking, back-broken bondservants to worship God in a land flowing with milk and honey. Moses was a leader in the truest sense of the word, a man designed to invoke change for Israel, to cast vision and initiate transformation through the power of the Almighty. Missing today in a majority of our churches is a similar type of leading with an equivalent quality of passion.

Leading Your Ministry is divided into three parts. Part 1 is an introduction into the emerging pastoral paradigm. No one alive today has witnessed such a significant shift in our concept of the local church pastor as we are presently undergoing. Perhaps not since the Reformation has our mental concept of the role of the clergy changed as it is today. This new paradigm is about pastors acting more like leaders than merely spiritual technicians and church managers.

Part 2 deals with a philosophy of leadership. Nearly all Christian books and most marketplace books on leadership discuss skills. Unfortunately, most do not provide the background that contextualize the skills. Without a proper understanding of why these tools work, many pastors are frustrated as they try the new implements. To present leadership ideas without sufficient explanation of the philosophy of leadership is much the same as teaching a person how to use a box of tools and then turning the mechanic loose on a malfunctioning car. It is one thing to know the tools; it is quite another to understand auto mechanics. This section deals with some of the big picture principles based on the emerging leadership paradigm of the twenty-first century. Not only is the pastorate changing, so is the process of leadership itself, throughout society.

Part 3 focuses on leadership skills. These chapters involve the more practical, how-to issues of being an effective leader as well as helping make leadership happen within your church, even if you are not a gifted leader by nature. The most vital elements for leading are addressed in order to help you cut through the many leadership concepts discussed in other literature.

This book is not a critique of what others have said about leadership, about their perceived strengths or shortcomings. The goal is to provide ideas that are emerging in the field of leadership studies and synthesize them with older concepts that are placed in the context of the congregation. Many books strive to explain leader traits and behaviors in hopes of instilling leadership abilities. This book is designed to help you understand the nature of leadership as much as possible in a pastoral context, so that you will begin to become a better church leader, and not just mimic leaderlike behaviors.

Today the temperature is rising. The bush is on fire again. Perhaps as never before, God is calling those who would be leaders to lead his people into new lands, to realize his promises. Now, as never before, the call is before us for men and women who would act like leaders, not just priests or prophets, not just spiritual technicians and church managers.

As the lay movement continues in what seems to be a re-reformation, laity are looking for pastors who would recruit, train, and motivate them to minister. Small congregations burdened with smaller budgets and dwindling resources will also be forced to equip and unleash the laity to carry on the work of God's kingdom. Pastors who want to bring about change among the 85 percent of dying or plateaued churches, and those who wish to raise up new congregations and lead large ones must retool.

This book is not for everyone. There are still a large number of pastors who are content to work out of the fading paradigm. There are certainly enough congregations that are willing to let the traditional pastor do the ministry for them. But this book is not for those people. This book is for lay leaders experiencing a growing dissatisfaction with pastors who are inclined to live one year after another without a sense of destiny or vision or burden of what God wants to see happen in their local parish.

Leading Your Ministry is likely to be read by those in pastoral ministry. However, there are a number of other ways in which this book can be used as it focuses on leadership from a twenty-first century mind-set. People in missions, non-profit, and parachurch ministries can benefit from the concepts. We hope denominational leaders and ministerial preparation professors will use this as a teaching text. Those in government and the business marketplace can glean from the principles as well. Leadership tends to be somewhat generic. The difference is how and where it is applied.

Perhaps the best way to use this book is among lay leaders who with the pastor can brainstorm about implementing this emerging paradigm. By using this as a leadership training tool, a team of people can grow together to discuss it and hold each other accountable. Since leadership is about people coming together to name mutual dreams and accomplish joint goals, may God's blessings multiply as you strive to serve and expand God's kingdom.

The times are changing. The bush burns bright. The bush burns hot. Take off your sandals. Listen intently. God may be calling your name as the next leader for a group of people, ready to be released for ministry and liberated from the chains of tradition and the games of playing church. If so, lead with passion.

PART ONE
THE NEW PASTORAL PARADIGM

CHAPTER 1

RETOOL OR RETIRE

N ear the turn of the twentieth century, horse-drawn-buggy factories faced contemporary threats as the horseless carriage
rumbled into existence. Many said that little would come of the
modern contraptions. "If man were meant to travel so fast without the aid
of an animal, God would have built us that way." In spite of the jesting,
Ford and others built their cars. Within a few short years, factories and
tradesmen who did not retool in response to the booming automobile
industry faced forced retirement. Similar stories continued through the
years so that today in certain fields, retooling has become a standard
operating procedure.

Those of us who offer services to congregations might snub our noses
at such stories, believing that our trade (and our guilds) will forever be
the same. We sympathize with our sisters and brothers who are forced to
change due to technological breakthroughs or shifting patterns in the
culture, but we doers of ministry assume that we are immune from such
transformations. If our only assignment were to explain "theology" (and
not necessarily to anyone else but ourselves), such an attitude might be
acceptable. But as soon as we add people to the formula, our roles also
become susceptible to drastic changes.

The auto and buggy exist for the same purpose—transportation. Transportation has not changed. It involves the process of getting people from
one place to another. The basic purpose of the church is not likely to

change—getting people into service and worship of God. However, as the people dynamics change, the way we "do business" is apt to require transformation. The face of the pastorate is changing. With a large majority of our churches "dying for change" and the perceived number of clergy on the verge of burning out and calling it quits, one might note that something needs to change. The mental concept of an ordained person feeding, shepherding, counseling, and basically running the church is fading. A growing number of parishioners are looking for something else in a pastor. Some of them have articulated this. Most have not, but they sense the tension. Doing business as usual in the church is not cutting it as we enter the twenty-first century.

Like the buggy builders and so many who have followed, we must be willing to retool—or we can retire. Although there will probably be a place in the future for the stereotypical pastor-shepherd, the places for these roles are diminishing. Although the inherent spiritual and social needs of people will never change, the dynamics in society today are calling for a different sort of pastor. Those of us in ministry or preparing for the ministry have two options; we can shake our fists at the prophets of change, much like the buggy manufacturers did a century ago, or we can face the music and prepare for the inevitable future in the church.

The Paradigm Shift

"Having spent much of the last decade researching organizational behavior and ministry impact, I am convinced that there are just a handful of keys to successful ministry. One of the indispensable characteristics of a ministry that transforms lives is leadership. This may sound simplistic. Unfortunately, relatively few churches actually have a leader at the helm. In striving to understand why most churches in this country demonstrate little positive impact on people's lives, I have concluded that it is largely due to the lack of leadership."[1]

George Barna points out that less than 4 percent of all senior pastors can communicate a clear vision for their ministry, a major component in leadership. He also notes that nearly a fourth of all pastors failed to identify their spiritual gifts, and only 6 percent of all senior pastors identified with having the gift of leadership. This compares with over half who identified teaching and preaching gifts. "The churches we have studied that are facilitating significant spiritual development within their people are pastored by those who claim the gift of leadership in their gift mix."[2]

This desire for pastors who would act more like leaders, and less like either traditional resident theologians or parish managers, reflects a major pastoral paradigm shift. A paradigm has to do with a pattern of thinking, a conceptual backdrop for perceived reality. When Copernicus suggested that the earth was not the center of the universe, this created a new paradigm, a new worldview. When Jesus revealed a personal path to God through his death and resurrection, this gave us a new spiritual/theological paradigm. A paradigm tends to be a large framework by which we perceive reality and organize new ideas.

Until recently, the roles of the pastorate appeared to remain basically unscathed by social changes. The pastor since the Reformation has been much the same, a person who ran the operations of a congregation, who preached the Word, counseled people, and basically managed the religious organization on the neighborhood corner or at the intersections of Main Street.

Not since the Reformation have we undergone such a dramatic change in the role of the clergy. Just after Luther posted his theses, congregational shepherds went through a major self-image adjustment. No longer were they the go-betweens for God and the people, the sellers of indulgences and the holy head over the lowly laity. The new pastor was much more common, more focused on teaching the Word so that all could understand. The new pastoral paradigm changed the local cleric's name from priest to parson, pastor, or just preacher. This historical event would forever affect how the local parish saw its leader. A transformation had taken place. Little has changed since the seventeenth century in terms of the overall pastoral paradigm.

The days when the pastor serves solely as resident theologian, teacher, counselor, and church manager are quickly passing. Now people are looking for those who are not only equipped for ministry but who also act like leaders. Up to this point the pastor was the leader simply because of his title and his position. However, most pastors were never really expected or allowed to actually lead. Now, with the changing times, we are expecting more from our "leaders" than sermons, budget setting, and policy maintenance. We are looking for those who will also set vision and significantly move the church forward. The problem is that most pastors are schooled and molded out of the old paradigm where few taught or seriously thought about leadership. The way we as pastors do business is changing just as so many other professions in the world. We can curse the change and buck it, longing for the good ol' days, or we can face reality and retool for the new times.

Causes of the "Leadership Dilemma"

Unless you have been living in a cave or have insulated yourself from the marketplace you have heard a growing number of people crying for more and better leaders from the world in general and the church in particular. Since ministry has to do with meeting the needs of people, we need to understand the social pressures people in general are experiencing

1. *Our civilization is undergoing incredible changes.* Things are not like they used to be. They never are. But things are more different today than they have ever been. The element of change itself has become a cultural constant. Change used to be the exception to the rule. It is the new rule. The momentum of the rate of change has not crescendoed. The incredible increase of discoveries, social transitions, technological inventions, and corporate upheavals are producing more changes than at any other time in history. The people in our churches and communities feel these changes, some subtle, some very obvious. Of these changes listed, probably the most significant is technology. The Information Age has created an inordinate number of possibilities in terms of work, urbanization, communication, education, and all that these entail. Life will never be the same as we continue to see changes happen more and faster every year.

Change creates stress. During times of stress and change, we seek leaders. Unfortunately, the fast pace of change has not necessarily shown us where we are headed. We are only traveling faster. The mere speed of the pace makes us more anxious to know where it is we are headed so fast. Leaders help us cope with stress and organization. They direct us. Perhaps there are not fewer leaders than before, but we sense a need for more and better leaders. The present demand is greater than the supply.

2. *Institutions have not provided for leadership training.* Our model of seminary training for persons in ordained ministry, dating back to the middle of the nineteenth century has remained much the same, even though society has changed by leaps and bounds. The context in which theology and Bible are taught has changed. Some schools respond with more practical courses such as church management, counseling, worship leading, and boardroom functioning, but these are not getting at the heart of leadership. One reason for the low supply of leaders is that we have rarely emphasized principles of leading, of influencing people toward change, in our preparation programs.

The words *leader* and *leadership* are quite common in educational advertising. However, they occur less among the actual college catalogs and course descriptions, and rarely do these words show up in classes. In essence, the course contents are not matching our claims. There is a big difference between teaching those in leadership positions how to preach homiletically correct sermons, and teaching pastors how to lead people. Academics defend the present programs by saying that there is no room within the present learning tracks to present leadership courses. "Such electives are viable, but not at the sake of theology, languages, homiletics, etc." By this prioritization, the idea is communicated that leadership is not essential in the pastorate.

3. *The fragmentation of society has made leadership much more difficult.* John Gardner suggests that one of the reasons for our lack of leaders is that society as we know it has become fragmented, making it more difficult to lead than ever before. We have varying loyalties often in conflict with one another. Our pluralistic society allows for the idea of multiple "truths."

The disintegration of the extended family unit is perhaps the primary source of the many organizational instabilities. Leadership is a communal experience. The lack of community in our society today—which is manifest simultaneously with the breakdown of family systems—makes leading harder than ever, yet we are also in a time when we need it more than ever.

4. *Leadership paradigms have changed.* A more subtle reason for the perceived shortage of leaders is that the concept of leadership itself is changing. Previous generations provided for more obvious leaders due to the Great Man theory. This sort of leadership was more hierarchical, top-down, authoritarian, and dramatic. It represented an industrial era mind-set. Now that we are in the postindustrial age, the style of leading is taking on a kinder, gentler approach. Twenty-first century leadership is more apt to involve interdependence, sensitivity to people, and sharing of ideas and information. This does not imply weaker leaders, rather leaders who are more relational and less autocratic. Therefore, the leaders may be less obvious in that they do not reflect the old stereotype of a boisterous, dictatorial leader standing alone.

5. *Leaders are feeling higher demands and fewer rewards.* The cost of effective leading is high, but there is the perception that, especially in the church, the rewards often do not outweigh the costs. Leaders by their very nature tend to receive criticisms and adversarial encounters and must make tough decisions. Most do not receive the pay, perks, or recognition that would help create a balance for this sense of giving. Perhaps this sounds crass and humanistic, but a growing number of denominational leaders acknowledge the shortage of capable pastors who would lead our more demanding churches. When a challenge to leading takes place in the church, which is intended to be a refuge of love, faith, and hope, and where finances and resources are almost always bordering on extinction, the payoffs may not seem significant enough to attract the best and brightest.

The perception of the pastor today has lost some of its glory. Between the secularization of America, the televangelist scandals, and the consumerism within churches, there is the tendency for us to lower our evaluation of pastors. The expectations and criticisms have increased, while the tangible and intangible benefits have decreased. This has helped deter some of our finest talent from seriously considering a call to the ministry.

Causes for the Pastoral Paradigm Shift

The same people undergoing societal stress are the ones who come to our churches, looking for spiritual direction addressing these anxieties. Though content at one time with a pastor who would theologize, shepherd, and counsel, these people now want a leader who would lead them out of the wilderness. Aside from the overall leadership dilemma in society and its effect of creating a desire for pastors who would lead, there are other influences that help us understand why the role of the minister is changing toward a leader pastor.

1. *Rise of the lay movement.* In addition to responding to a new social climate, the idea of lay ministry has required pastors to become trainers of leaders. During the 1970s and 1980s, the teaching of spiritual gifts significantly increased the awareness that there is a place for the ministry of the laity in the Body of Christ. A cadre of diagnostic instruments, seminars, and books are currently available to help cast the vision that laypeople are to be active components in the ministry of the congregation. From this teaching comes the idea that laypeople are called to minister. Therefore, someone must train and recruit them to be a part of the church staff.

During this same time, the small group movement rose considerably. People began taking Paul Cho's model seriously and westernized it for American use. Ministries like Serendipity and publications such as *Discipleship Journal* provide a support system of resources for developing and maintaining small groups. This is carried further by the recent move toward the metachurch model, defined by Carl George. The metachurch model is based on the concept that a church functions as a collage of small groups. The primary care of the people is via small groups so that mass worship services are a small group convention where everyone comes together, but then disperses again throughout the week into groups of four to fifteen people.

The staffing of small groups comes by way of the teaching of spiritual gifts, that every member has a ministry. Small groups open up a multitude of opportunities and needs for facilitating large numbers of people. A traditional church with Sunday school and worship has a limited number of ministry positions. For example, even in large churches, only a small percentage of people with gifts of teaching have the opportunity to teach because many of the classes are quite large. In a small group oriented body, there are numerous outlets for those with the gift of teaching. Every small group that has Bible study as a part of its purpose could use someone with this gift. Teaching is just one example of how the small group movement mushrooms the opportunities for the laity to carry on the business of the church which is ministry. Pastors must move from hands-on ministry to equipping, to being a leader of the ministers.

2. *Aging baby boomers.* The lay ministry movement primarily began in the 1970s, picked up speed in the 1980s, and is starting to explode in the 1990s. An important reason for this emphasis in the United States is a critical number of baby boomers who are reaching midlife. The books and focus on the post–World War II generation consisting of over 76 million Americans born between 1946 and 1964 are many. This generation is more unique from its preceding generation than perhaps any in history. The sheer size as well as the added elements of technology, advanced industrialization and urbanization, education, rising economics and improved financial status after the war, rock music, and marketing frenzy have given this generation a flavor very distinct from the tastes of its parents.

In the 1990s, the boomers started to hit the midlife transition in large numbers. At midlife, people begin thinking more about the time they have left. They start becoming frustrated with the fulfillment of acquisitions and status and start looking for deeper issues. A more conservative mind-set prevails. At the turn of the 1990s, a new spirit was sensed in our nation. We started caring about our environment and about leaving a world intact for our children. We recycle and McDonald's goes back to paper products instead of styrofoam. We show concern about our health, so we create non-fat, low-fat products. The boomers vote in their own president early on, but then replace a large number of liberal politicians for more conservative ones. Covers of national magazines start talking to us about our concern for spiritual things. The "s" words like *sin, spirituality,* and *supernatural* are now okay to discuss. A prolific interest in angels is taking place.

This reality check at midlife spawns a spiritual awakening. We see the men's movement start in the secular realm, followed by a Christian men's movement exemplified in Promise Keepers. Promise Keepers is the result of a critical number of men reaching midlife and wanting more in life. They realize they have been climbing the corporate ladder only to find it leaning against the wrong wall. They start becoming concerned about their family relationships and their friendships with other males. Midlife men start realizing that they will not live forever, and they want to experience life beyond their jobs. Promise Keepers is a modern example of what can happen when people are ripe for God to do something new in their midst.

One of the unique things about boomers is that they tend to be experiential in their orientation. Mix this with a rise in spirituality—and the result is lay ministry. We are now in such a reformation that a critical mass of people are saying, "I want to experience ministry, but I need help in finding a place."

3. *Large church preference.* Recent studies show that over 50 percent of total church attendance is in one-seventh of the churches. That means that the large churches are carrying more and more of the ministry load. A church of several hundreds and even thousands used to be a rarity, but it is now quite common from the center city to the urban communities.

This movement toward larger congregations will continue to increase as urban life continues to diminish rural possibilities. Like it or not, boomers are consumers. They will go where they can find the best service available, regardless of denominational heritage. They like options, and they want special ministries and programs designed to meet their unique needs. Small churches just cannot provide the supermarket-like array of spiritual and social products. Therefore, the boomer generation has tended toward pooling its resources around larger ministries, which can by sheer size in staff and budgets, provide for more fulfilling ministries.

Another reason for the desire for more specialized ministries in the congregation is that our society is growing increasingly complex. In the Ozzie and Harriet Nelson days of the more traditional, stable family, the needs tended to be somewhat simplified. There was the need for spiritual edification, occasional marriage counseling, and periodic crisis intervention. As societal violence, immorality, broken homes, drug abuse, and job insecurity escalates, dysfunctional people with diverse problems proliferate. Larger churches are best resourced to provide for an array of need-meeting ministries addressing single parenting, blended families, cancer support group, divorce recovery, and the spectrum of recovery options, not to mention the normal age group ministries and spiritual growth options. The diversity of felt needs makes churches that can offer help in these areas more attractive.

The size of these churches require pastors who must get beyond the personal touch model and basically provide leadership for expanding ministries. In addition, staff members of large churches find themselves needing to recruit and work through other people in order to respond to the growing demands of the larger crowds. These require more of a leader orientation, although many large churches become managerial after awhile. The ratio of total attendance with the smaller number of churches is likely to grow, also increasing the need for those who can lead various ministries instead of providing the personalized care directly.

Pastoral Ramifications

What does all of this mean for those of us who have been trained to be the primary ministry doers? It means that we are being called to move over and make room for a whole host of "amateur" pastors. It means that our role is changing from being the primary caregiver to becoming the trainer, recruiter, and equipper of many caregivers. Most ministry tends to be an end in itself. The ministry of leading is a means to an end. The dynamics continue to change as our churches move from a spectator orientation, where a few activists nurture the rest, to a larger number of members sharing in mutual ministry. Who is going to organize, train, and hold these ministers accountable? How is our own self-image as pastors going to change as we are expected to let others into what we were trained and taught to do—even on Sunday morning? How much humble self-confidence does it take to allow a layperson to "preach"? What new skills do we need to possess that we were not taught in college and seminary? These questions open the door to a whole new paradigm for congregations.

CHAPTER 2

THE JETHRO PRINCIPLE:
LEADING VERSUS MINISTERING

O ne of the earliest leadership consultants gave Moses some good advice.

"What you are doing is not good. You and these people who come to you will only wear yourselves out. The work is too heavy for you; you cannot handle it alone. Listen now to me and I will give you some advice, and may God be with you. . . . Select capable men from all the people . . . and appoint them as officials over thousands, hundreds, fifties and tens. Have them serve as judges for the people at all times, but have them bring every difficult case to you. . . . That will make your load lighter, because they will share it with you. If you do this and God so commands, you will be able to stand the strain, and all these people will go home satisfied." (Exod. 18:17-23)

Moses, perhaps the greatest example of a leader in the Bible, had succumbed to the day-in-and-day-out work of ministry. His role had changed from casting the vision of entering the promised land and fighting pharaohs to fixing people's problems on a personal level. His heart was right, his intentions sincere. But Moses had exchanged his leading for activities of ministry.

On the eventful day when Moses' father-in-law came to see him, Jethro's advice moved Moses from minister to leader again. His task as leader this time was different. Instead of liberating the people from Egypt, he began to liberate the people to minister to each other. That is a primary task of the pastor who would lead—not to provide hands-on care for each parishioner but to liberate the church to minister to itself. This allows the pastor the opportunity to lead while the church receives spiritual growth and thorough pastoral care. Most pastors are so consumed with doing ministry that they have little time left for leading.

The New Testament version of the Jethro principle is found in Acts 6, where the apostles found ministers who would feed the widows. Most pastors find themselves doing the hands-on work of ministry because the work of recruiting, equipping, and motivating ministers is a much harder task. If it were not, we would see it happening on a much broader scale.

Every pastor knows that a community's ministry opportunities are endless. Our time will always run out before the needs of the people are depleted. Trying to provide personal ministry in the typical congregation can lead to burnout mixed with feelings of anger, guilt, and inadequacy. Books and articles addressing this phenomenon are growing. Understanding the difference between ministry in general and the ministry of leading will tremendously expand your ministry capabilities.

The Emerging Paradigm

There is no clear pastoral model in the Bible. The early church was just emerging as the New Testament ends. The paradigm we know today has come to us from years of tradition and evolution. Humankind's basic needs are the same, but the structure in which those needs are met and the social contexts are much different than they were 1900 years ago. We can never go back to Palestinian times, and we should avoid the romantic notion that we must. Rather, we want to be a spirit-filled church in the twenty-first century. The type of church we are to be in the twenty-first century is also a different church than we were in the 1950s, which for all practical purposes is the model a majority of churches emulate today.

The movements toward small groups, lay ministry, and pastors as leaders are interrelated. Most churches have a limited number of ministry roles in their current structure. In the old paradigm we discover spiritual gifts (if we are progressive) so that we can recruit workers to teach Sunday school, serve on the greeter team, or function as a finance committee member. The problem with this is that you quickly run out of jobs that people want or that actually match a gift. The mind-set of helping people fill existing holes in the church ministry is limited.

A church that seriously considers the biblical premise for the priesthood of all believers changes its philosophy of doing business. The idea of teaching, discovering, and developing spiritual gifts is for the purpose of putting the entire church to work. We start matching gifts with needs in existing ministries, but we do not stop there. When a number of people are excited to serve but few outlets exist, it frustrates them. Rather, the church staff must see one of its primary roles as opening up new places for ministry. An entrepreneurial mind-set takes place whereby new ministries are created inside the church so people can find a place for ministry. The pastoral staff helps create opportunities for the purpose of allowing people a place to minister so that they can continue to grow spiritually.

When people are spectators watching a few trained people perform for them, they will be dwarfed in their spiritual formation. You never see a picture of a working fishing boat on the Dead Sea. The Dead Sea receives good water, but because there is no outlet which would allow for aeration, the water cannot support life. Christians who become mere receivers of ministry soon stagnate in their spiritual journey. The idea of staff becoming recruiters, trainers, and developers of new ministry opportunities is a leader mentality. The idea of merely holding the fort and staffing existing ministries is a managerial mentality.

Another limitation of the old church paradigm is that we see ministry as what takes place within the walls of the church. We assume that the only time we are really making a difference for the kingdom of heaven is when we are in some specifically sanctioned church program. People hold the concept that they need to go to church to do ministry, that it usually takes one to four hours, and that it should be listed in the Sunday bulletin calendar of events. In Exodus 19 and 1 Peter 2, where the church is referred to as a royal priesthood and a nation of priests, the context of the priest is to help people know God. God exhorted all of Israel, not just the pastoral tribe of Levi, to be a nation of priests. He did this after Moses learned the lesson of giving up the ministry. More pastors should get out of the ministry and get into leading, enabling the church to respond to its calling.

When we recognize that God expects all of us to serve him wherever we live, work, shop, play, and socialize, we start to look for his hand in our everyday life. We come to see more ministry as more convenient, something which God brings across our path when and where he wants us to be Jesus with skin on to others. All of a sudden, people see the importance of praying about changing jobs, buying houses, and using leisure time. Our main purpose in life is not just to make money and have fun on weekends. Our primary calling is to minister, to be priests wherever God calls us. Our work arena is our mission field. Our neighbors are our parishioners, and our social circles become our congregations.

When laity start seeing themselves as ministers of the gospel, they begin to eliminate the double standards they have for themselves and their pastors. They start to realize that they are held accountable for what they do, say, think, and believe. They expect their pastors to live holy lives, but they start to realize that it is their mission as well. There will not be two lines to get into heaven, clergy and laity. There will only be one—ministers of the gospel of Jesus Christ. For too long, many laity have hidden behind the excuse of not being called into the ministry, so they can live irresponsibly and avoid the need to grow spiritually. At the same time, they wonder why they struggle for a sense of significance in what they do. They search to find more fulfillment in the seemingly mundane tasks of everyday living. The philosophy of the priesthood of believers is full of great potential to bring about more holy and fulfilled living.

Ministry is an act of dispensing God's grace. "Apart from me," Jesus said, "you can do nothing." When we minister, we are merely letting God's grace flow through us, so that we are vessels in God's service. The elitism often found among clergy gives the impression that there are special grace dispensers. My grandmother used to collect saltshakers. Some of them were beautiful crystal and silver shakers. But when I wanted salt for a green apple or rhubarb stalk, I did not care whether that salt came from a crystal shaker or a salt box. In acts of mercy we need to help people distinguish between the salt and the dispenser. When we confuse the two, we start to elevate one dispenser over other dispensers. The role of the clergy is not to be elevated above other grace dispensers, but it is to train and recruit others to be the best dispensers they can become. This requires very confident pastors who are willing to work themselves out of jobs.

The bottom line is that God calls all people, not just the clergy, to serve as priests, pastors, and chaplains in various social circles. The spiritual gift passages (1 Corinthians 12, Romans 12, Ephesians 4) give us the impression that our gifts are to edify other Christians, but the Bible never suggests we relegate our activities solely to the organized church. To grasp this concept, we need pastors who will help laity in their spiritual formation by providing resources and an environment where they can grow spiritually.

The Leader as Part of the Body

First Corinthians 12 and similar passages in the New Testament, describe spiritual gifts and various roles Christians perform as parts of the Body. One or more of these roles involves leading. If we are to trust these passages, it is ludicrous to suggest that everyone can be a leader, because all are not so endowed. God gives us special graces (charisma) to perform specific tasks and to help the whole Body function with health. A leader who is doing her job under the gift of God's Spirit is important, but no more important than a nonleader who is doing what she is gifted to do. Scriptures say that all of the parts have value in the body, not just those who lead.

Those who suggest that leaders are everything tend to overestimate their importance while underestimating the valuable roles of nonleaders. As a pastor, I am no better than anyone else in my church, just because my role requires me to lead. By leading I am "just doing my job," similar to when a singer sings and a teacher teaches. The hierarchical view of leadership suggests that the pastor is more important than the janitor or Sunday school worker. This ought not to be so. At the same time, those of us who are gifted and called to lead should go at it with confidence and assertiveness, just as each should perform his or her role in the Body of Christ with excellence.

Due to the vital role of the leader, when he is not doing his job, the body greatly suffers as a whole, much the same way that our physical body suffers greatly when the head has a concussion. A concussion can render the body useless. Many ecclesiastical "vegetables" exist where the body is basically functioning, but little dynamic life is evident. When I do what I refer to as a "paralysis analysis" of a dysfunctional organization, the first thing I look at is the effectiveness of leadership.

Leading is a ministry, but not all ministry is leading. If a pastor is expected to lead, we refer to him as the leader. However, we are mistaken when we assume that all his ministry has to do with leadership. There are many ways a pastor ministers which have little or nothing to do with leading. Therefore, when you lead out of service for Christ you are ministering, but certainly all ministry is not leading and does not pertain to leadership. When we confuse leading with other types of ministry or ministry in general, leadership becomes confusing and difficult to understand.

Leading, Ministry, Managing

There are three basic categories of pastoral behaviors and expectations. The first is ministry, or what we might call spiritual provision. This includes religious activities such as serving the sacraments, teaching, preaching, counseling, prayer, evangelism, discipleship, making hospital calls, marrying and burying. The second category has to do with management, which includes organizational facilitation such as board meetings, daily administration, budgeting and finances, and program assistance. The third category is leadership. Most category one and two activities are not leadership, even though a leader can lead by way of a ministry like preaching (i.e., vision casting) or chairing a board meeting (i.e., setting policy).

By far, theological education focuses on laying a foundation for the first category. There is a vast array of literature available on spiritual provision spanning from theology to biblical studies, from counseling to homiletic books and articles. A contemporary movement called practical theology seeks to apply the first and train in the second (management). Leadership training is practically nonexistent.

Many who design pastoral programs and ministry seminars refer to them as "leadership training." But there is a difference between leadership training where training is the noun and leadership is the adjective, and the training of leaders where training is the verb and leader is the noun. What many refer to as leadership training has little or nothing to do with teaching pastors or laity how to lead. Rather, it often refers to training those we call leaders in any number of skills such as church growth, preaching, counseling, and so forth. By referring to ministry aspects as leadership training, we deceive ourselves in presuming that we are teaching people about leading. The training of those in leadership roles is not the same as training people to understand leadership. You can teach would-be leaders any number of skills such as praying, marketing, leading small groups, and theology, without even touching leadership concepts. The way many use the term, you could gather a group of pastors (leaders) and teach them basket weaving and call it leadership training.

A pastor is the one who is most responsible for the product of the church, which is primarily various forms of ministry. The problem is in thinking of the pastor as the primary or even sole source of ministry. A leader realizes that she is not to be the sole source of the local ministry, but is the most responsible for making sure it happens. In essence, it is important that one learns to distinguish between leading and feeding. A leader need not feed, but must make sure feeding takes place.

Just because the pastor is the most responsible person in a church does not mean that he will lead or that his leading will be effective. There are some wonderful churches around the country where the pastors are not so much leaders as they are feeders and managers. Growth can emerge out of a great talent used by God or a special anointing. Scores of people can be helped, but the effectiveness of the church rests largely on the individual talent of the pastor. Leadership seeks to create an empowered body. Feeding attracts consumers. Leadership develops workers because it involves a number of people working together. A leader helps catalyze leadership.

Spiritual Technicians

A minister is a spiritual technician. He is the one who personally carries out the ministry task. Most pastors grew up believing and being schooled to think that their primary job is to be spiritual technicians. A pastor is to know the ins and outs of marital counseling, performing rituals, officiating at services, and tinkering with homiletics, exegesis, and similar theological exercises. None of these skills are dispensable. However, a pastor can be very good at a mix of these skills and still fail to run the race due to a lack of leadership. There is a difference in being a trained professional to do the primary ministry of a local church and being a trained professional who acts as a resource center to recruit, motivate, equip, and organize the parts of the body to do their individual tasks. The goal of the leader is to unleash the church. Too many churches unleash the pastor to serve them as a spiritual technician. The new paradigm uses the pastor as a sort of spiritual foreman, responsible for supervising the technicians. Many church boards and influencers want to lead, so they hire the seminary trained technician to do what he does best, perform in religious activities.

Laypeople fail to see themselves as the spiritual technicians for three main reasons. The first is insecure pastors. Most pastors find a certain amount of fulfillment in being The Minister. Who can do ministry better than someone called by God and trained in undergraduate and graduate school? The pastor, unwilling to share the limelight or blessing of ministry and earnestly wanting to serve the people, assumes the role of spiritual technician. Soon she finds herself inundated with calls from people needing her services. This unwillingness to share ministry often comes out of an insecurity of the laity messing up the situation or dropping the ball, or worse, ministering better than the pastor. In order to avoid the mess and stress, pastors run to every ministry opportunity they see in the flock and create a dependent culture in the church. Insecure pastors need to be needed and therefore help produce an environment where they are seen as ministry messiahs, donning a cape with a big "M" and soaring off to respond to the congregation's dilemmas. Many counselors would call this codependency.

Pastors often joke about the multitudinous expectations parishioners have of them, including functions such as teacher, counselor, administrator, CEO, CFO, public relations spokesman, priest, janitor, preacher, fund-raiser, contractor, and so on. Considering that 85 percent of the churches in the United States average under 200 Sunday morning attenders, one can understand the breadth of these expectations in that little room exists for specialization in such an organization. The small church pastorate is one of the last generalist professions existing in a specialist's world. But what comes first, the small church or the pastor who serves as a minister versus a leader? Do pastors tend to behave as ministers because most churches are 200 or less in size and force them into this mold, or do most churches fail to grow beyond the 200 mark because most pastors would rather minister than lead? Since leadership is a cooperative venture, it is safe to say that the cause is multigenetic. However, pastors called and trained to lead generally lead their churches beyond the 200 mark and emphasize that ministry is primarily a function of the laity.

A second reason that the laity fail to see themselves as ministers is scriptural ignorance. God calls the Israelites to be a nation of priests. Someone said, "The laity are not in the church; they are not for the church; they don't do things at the church. They are the church." Jesus has called all believers to be fishers of people (Matt. 4:19). We are to be the light (Matt. 5:14). We are to be harvesters (Matt. 9:38). Peter says, "You also, like living stones, are being built into a spiritual house to be a holy priesthood, offering spiritual sacrifices acceptable to God through Jesus Christ. . . . You are a chosen people, a royal priesthood, a holy nation, a people belonging to God, that you may declare the praises of him who called you out of darkness into his wonderful light" (1 Pet. 2:5, 9). In Exodus 19:5-6 God says, "Now if you obey me fully and keep my covenant, then out of all nations you will be my treasured possession. Although the whole earth is mine, you will be for me a kingdom of priests and a holy nation." God was not speaking here to the Levites, the tribe of spiritual technicians, but to the entire nation. Scriptures are replete with the idea that all believers are called to be priests to their family, pastors at their office, chaplains to their neighborhood—ministers. By avoiding preaching and teaching on such scriptures, we remain ignorant to God's idea that all of us are "called" to minister.

A third reason why pastors have taken up the role as spiritual technician versus a foreman leading technicians is because the laity see his willingness to serve and use this as a way to avoid responsibility. We hire people to wash our cars, clean our clothes, school our children, cook and serve us food, and mow our yards. It only makes sense to hire someone else to do our ministry—enter the pastor. "He's trained. He has a heart for God. He has the time. Let him do it."

Some pastors say, "But my people don't want me to lead; they want me to minister." Resist this trap! The first job of the leader is to cast vision, to help the people see their potential and the objectives before them. Leaders are about change, and every congregation needs change, or you would not have been called or appointed there. When a church needs to change toward a biblical model of Christianity, where all the members are ministers, the pastor's job is to initiate this conversion. The outcome is the result of his effectiveness at leading. As long as I tied my son's shoe, he was more than happy not to learn to tie his own shoe. There finally came a point when I taught him that it was his job to tie his shoes, and that I would show him how and then expect him to tie them. At the same time, leadership is a relationship; leadership may prove ineffective if the parishioners are unwilling to make or move toward the changes. Even Jesus could not lead those who were unwilling to be led.

The leader must constantly ask the question, "Do I need to do this ministry or can I recruit, train, and unleash someone else?" The equipping pastor never does ministry alone. He is always training, motivating, and equipping the laity to minister. Effective leading emphasizes a team approach and works to organize the parts of the Body according to their gifts.

Multiplying Ministry

The Jethro Principle has to do with decentralizing the ministry focus and providing an array of ministry outlets to the people. We are so concerned that the quality of the care will diminish if we take it out of the pastor's hands. According to Exodus 18, the quality of the care improved as the number of ministry points increased. A church will usually cease growing when it is not able to provide individual pastoral care to its people. The reason most churches hover around the 100 mark in membership is because that is the number the average pastor can nurture by himself. Jethro suggested Moses find qualified leaders to oversee ten people each and then middle managers who would oversee larger numbers. This logarithmic breakdown allowed for a significant increase in ministry, centering around a small group network. Small groups serve two primary purposes. They provide pastoral care on an individual basis, while allowing for an increased number of ministry opportunities.

When the pastor is the primary caregiver, the ministry of the church will always be limited. If someone is in the hospital, the pastor goes for comfort. If counseling needs to be done, she becomes the therapist. When the building needs work, the pastor calls together the board to determine the action and may even volunteer or be expected to fix it herself. The pastor is the teacher, preacher, business manager, and she performs any number of other task-oriented activities. The key here is not that the leader pastor is unwilling to do these things, or that she is too important, but rather this is a misuse of the gifts of the pastor and laity. The bottom line is stewardship. Large churches often provide better care for their people in that they must rely on resources outside of a single pastor or set of pastors. Some large churches work out of the old paradigm when the staff basically specialize in areas of ministry. Large churches working out of the new pastoral paradigm will hire staff primarily for their ability to reproduce themselves and develop lay leaders and lay ministers who fulfill the ministry needs as well as their own callings. Most pastoral care is best served through a small group setting. A leader can know and care for a group of four to twelve people on a personal level.

Three Challenges in Taking the Plunge

Three inherent challenges arise in churches which begin buying into the priesthood of believers. One problem is the difference in quality of ministry between the professional and the amateur, so that people discredit that which comes from the lay minister. This problem is more of a leader issue. It signifies that the pastor has probably done a poor job in helping the person find a place of ministry reflective of his or her gifts and training that person sufficiently. Some pastors complain that the people just do not want to put in the time to be trained; but again, persuading and motivating tend to be leader issues.

Insecure pastors like the feeling of being needed. Codependent tendencies run high in the pastorate, where many find their identities and self-worth in helping those who need them. This dysfunctional attitude breeds the same in congregations, so that the pastor keeps the church dependent upon his ministry, thus validating his presence and hopefully guaranteeing his job. Secure pastors are willing to develop independent people. They encourage laity to take over ministries and take responsibility for their own spiritual growth. They preach the passages that advocate the priesthood of believers and the ministry of the Body to itself. Secure pastors constantly strive to work themselves out of jobs, understanding that there will always be a high demand for such leaders.

The second problem prevalent when one starts to promote the idea that laypeople are to be carrying out the bulk of ongoing ministry, is that other laypeople often do not want to accept the ministry of their peers. A part of the rejection is qualitative, as suggested above, but the other is perceptual. Because the old system elevates the grace which comes from the ordained grace dispensers, we invalidate that which comes from others. The old ways are so well established that even when we get people recruited and equipped to minister, others are often not receptive to their ministry. They still want the pastor to call on them in the hospital. "It's just not the same" when someone else loves them. We even see this hierarchy of divine grace dispensed in large churches, where the senior pastor is preferred over staff pastors, in instances such as baptism. One way to chip away at this pecking order is to quit using sermon illustrations about you personally bringing comfort to someone in the hospital or how you stayed up all night praying with a family for their child. This grandstanding echoes the idea that you are the savior of the church and the person to call when ministry is needed. Tell stories of laity acting like ministers. A part of leading in the new paradigm involves preparing the laity to receive ministry from itself and validate what God can and will do through those willing to serve.

A third challenge of any pastor who goes about making this ministry model shift is finding the time to recruit, train, and motivate while providing personal ministry to those expecting it. Any change in paradigms requires transitions. It's the transitions that do us in, more so than the changes. A transition is like a hallway. Halls lead from room to room but are not to be inhabited. Like Moses, most pastors are so busy addressing the needs of the people that they have little quality time to invest in those who would lighten their load. It is a "Catch-22" situation which keeps many pastors from ever becoming leaders. Start anyway. Carve out intentional times with key lay leaders for the purpose of discipling and then training them to serve as key ministers. (See figure 2a.)

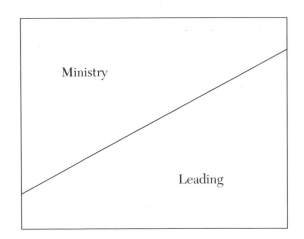

Figure 2a: Pastor Moving from Ministry to Leading

To begin, you spend a minority of your time in the leader/trainer role because you are busy functioning as a minister. As you can see by the graph, most of your efforts continue to focus out of a ministry mind-set. As you gradually gain those around you who are equipped to carry out the ministry to others, you can invest an increasing amount of time and energy focusing on training other ministers and leaders. Note the word *invest.*

Most ministry is not an investment. It is an expenditure. When Moses put time into recruiting and training those who would minister to the people, he invested in a process which yielded great rewards. Eventually, more of your time can be placed into the development of other ministers.

Toward the end of the transition, a majority of your time is spent developing other leaders who are in turn developing ministry teams which care for the needs of the church.

A pastor begins to measure the amount of leader activities he is involved in by listing his regular activities and labeling them, I, II, or III. Type III activities would consist of ministerial and managerial tasks such as sermon preparation, most board meetings, planning budgets, setting up rooms, hospital calls, discipleship, evangelism, and so on. Type II activities involve training people to minister, whether it be in seminars, one on one, or taking people with you to model as you minister. Type I activities deal directly with leading. Type IA has to do with personal leader behaviors such as brainstorming new ministries, vision casting, recruiting a leadership team, and so on. Type IB activities involve training of other leaders, whether it be discipling or nurturing potential leaders or discussing leadership principles with existing leaders. The purpose is for intentional leadership development. A brief but thorough analysis of a typical pastor's week would reveal a heavy dose of Type III duties and very few Type I activities.

In this model, the pastor basically works herself out of a job as a minister. She continues to perform ministry tasks from time to time, but they are threefold. First of all, there will likely be some uncovered areas from time to time that the pastor will need to cover since she is most responsible for making sure ministry takes place. These are rarities in the effectively led church. The second area requiring her to minister as a leader pastor is when she ministers as a model for training others. The third and primary reason a leader pastor will minister is to care for the other leaders. Someone needs to pastor the pastors so that they continue to be nurtured on a personal level. The pastor will always be a minister, although her flock will change from the sheep to the shepherds.

New paradigm pastors unleash the church into the community, in both formal and informal ministry. Leaders help people feel good about their work in the kingdom of heaven whether or not it takes place in the church building. When we start using paid staff and ministry directors to recruit, train, and motivate for ministry within and beyond the walls of the church, we are really developing a leader oriented approach.

Mind of a Priest, Soul of a Prophet

A clear biblical model that best fits a pastor is difficult to find. Leaders in the Bible were often not priests. For example, David was a great leader who knew God personally, but he was not a temple priest. The pastor of a congregation is a type of modern priest. He is the chief teacher, the spiritual leader, and one who carries out many of the religious practices expected of the local priest. That is why, for the most part, pastors are not business leaders who take time out to do their spiritual responsibilities. Even bivocational pastors think of themselves as pastors first, who have to support themselves financially with tent-making jobs.

Most priests are more like spiritual technicians than they are leaders. They fulfill the obligations of weekly temple activities and special holiday services. Their goals tend to be more maintenance than expansion. On the other hand, prophets were voices for God who would announce "thus says the Lord." These prophetic leaders were visionary and motivational in their style. They saw what needed to be changed and sought to do what was necessary to change it. They acted like spiritual and social catalysts. By heart they were much more leaderlike in style than priests. However, many prophets behaved like Lone Rangers. They tended toward eccentric lifestyles even though they had an organized support group who cheered their actions. Although often good at casting vision, it would be difficult to suggest that the typical prophetic personality would fit the leadership qualifications in terms of empowerment and organizing toward intentional change. That responsibility was generally left to the ruler or similar governmental leader.

What seems to be needed today are pastors who have the mind of a priest and the soul of a prophet. Deep within the priestly personality must beat the heart of a prophet, one who hears from God and who is willing to announce, "thus says the Lord." This person is able to see what needs to change for things to be as God desires and is willing to take the necessary risks, the sort of risk taking that is capable of moving the hearts and actions of others. This person is not alienated from the crowds, but works in the institutions to bring about positive change. The pastor's job is to comfort the afflicted and afflict the comfortable. Such a hybrid pastor would seek to bring about revolutionary changes while being tuned into the ongoing needs of the people, realizing that people seek someone to stir the pot and lead the way.

PART TWO
A PHILOSOPHY
OF LEADERSHIP

CHAPTER 3

LEADERSHIP FOR THE
TWENTY-FIRST CENTURY

Coming to Terms with the Terms

Two elderly women were sitting on the front porch one late summer evening. The crickets were chirping and the sound of a church choir could be heard down the street. One woman said, "Isn't that sound heavenly?"

The other replied, "Yes, and to think they do that by rubbing their legs together."

We all know the difficulty of communicating when both parties are talking about different things.

"Anyone can be a leader."

"Let's play follow-the-leader."

"I'm the leader here. Now everyone, settle down!"

"Everything rises and falls on leadership."

"Take me to your leader."

"Managers do things right. Leaders do the right things."

"Leaders are made, not born."

"If the followers lead; the leaders will follow."

"He's the worship leader. She's the children's leader. And I'm the small group leader."

All too often, we assume that by using the same words, we are talking about the same thing. Homiletics, hermeneutics, translations versus paraphrases, and theological terms are all important in traditional ministerial training. A lot of people, however, who write and talk about leaders and leadership never get around to defining the terms. In theology, that would be like a Methodist, a Jehovah's Witness, and a Mormon having a discussion about God and Jesus Christ. The terminology might sound the same, but they would be talking about different belief systems. Pastors are taught that contextualization of their message is essential. In a similar manner, whenever you hear the terms *leader* and *leadership*, you must look at the context in which they are used.

Now that leadership is such a hot topic, it is very tempting to throw it around wherever it might sound good. Everyone seemingly likes the thought of being a leader and preparing leaders. Seminars emerge touting the secrets of leading. Graduate and doctor of ministry programs announce their emphasis in leadership. We title church journals "Leadership," promoting the idea that pastors need to be leaders, or assuming they are leaders. We add the words "leader" and "leadership" to countless courses, books, tapes, and people jump onto the bandwagon to explain this complex and difficult process. Teachers of workshops and classes throw the word *leadership* into subjects on worship, preaching, prayer, youth ministry, and any number of other themes. A large percentage of authors intermix leadership with topics such as management, ministry skills, and spiritual formation. Most fall far short in the endeavor of explaining leadership and developing leaders who lead confidently. The rising levels of frustration among pastors and congregations are often the result of so much confusion in this area.

Biblical Leadership?

Currently I have over two hundred volumes on leadership in my personal library and the number grows monthly. Over one-fourth of these books are from a Christian perspective. It appears that on the topic of leadership, we Christians have kept the pace with those in business and secular fields.

Some Christians have not kept pace, thinking that the Bible is a manual for leaders. That is a problematic way of thinking. The Bible was not intended to be a leadership text, even though it illustrates the concept through many of its stories.

A majority of Christian leadership literature tends to do one or more of three things with the Bible. First, many authors determine to study the people in the Bible who were apparently leaders, such as Moses, Deborah, David, Esther, Nehemiah, Paul, and others, suggesting that most of the things they did depict leading. The problem with this imposition on the text is that these persons were not local church pastors, and so our context is different. Furthermore, everything that a leader does is not involved with leading. A leader can teach, manage, counsel, and pray; but these activities are not necessarily leading. Therefore, it is dangerous to watch a "leader" and assume that we can learn about leading, for that person may not be leading at the time. We erroneously impose many other behaviors and teachings upon the subject of leadership which often do not belong. The stories of biblical leaders include some leadership behaviors and principles here and there, but the chronicles are not meant for leadership studies. Therefore, we tend to either force the scriptures to fit our leadership paradigms or we strain the scriptures by striving to read leadership into passages which were never intended to teach us about leadership.

The second popular approach to leadership via the Scripture is to investigate the very brief characteristics required for early church elders in the Pauline Epistles. We see minimal church structure during the early church. Although delegation began in Acts 6, and bishops and elders were denoted by 1 Timothy, little is given in terms of the nature of leadership and the behaviors of leaders. Therefore, many experts give a long list of character expectations that pertain to leaders. These expectations are little more than qualities that you would expect from any growing and mature Christian, whether a leader or not. Leaders should, of course, understand and implement mature character traits more than others, both to model as well as to withstand the pressures of leadership. However, characteristics such as love, servanthood, the fruit of the spirit, perseverance, and being filled with the Holy Spirit are not evidence of leadership. They are Christian behaviors.

A third problem with searching Scripture to determine leadership principles is cultural and historical differences. Most leadership books and materials today are developed from a Western mind-set, with metaphors from industry and commerce, politics and law. Although the goals of leadership may be similar from culture to culture, namely that leadership is a process whereby people work together to accomplish goals, the goals and manner in which the process takes place varies. Those of us from the West and especially the United States tend to be ethnocentric. We presume that reality works out of our cultural paradigm. Leadership in the United States is often different than it is in an Asian, African, or mid-Eastern culture. Obviously, the Scriptures were not written from a Western mind-set. Unless we study the original languages and cultural context of Bible times, we miss hidden meanings. Translators work hard to bring about bridges for us to walk across in order to understand these messages. When we strive to force a Western mind-set of leadership into an ancient Near Eastern context as depicted in the Scripture, we do an injustice to ourselves and the Bible.

Formal leadership studies did not begin until 1900, and in-depth emphasis on leadership did not take off until the 1970s and 1980s. In fact, the word *leadership* itself only dates back a century or two. The concept of leading is not new. Leadership has no doubt been a part of civilization as long as groups have formed to achieve things together. However, the formal study of the concept is relatively new. Except for a few books such as Machievelli's *Prince* and some Asian military strategy manuals, little exists along the line of historical leadership literature. What may seem to be quite common to us is relatively new in terms of history. Therefore, to place our paradigm onto literature that was not written for such a perspective is improper if not reckless. Results of doing this are at best patchy and often wear thin on the integrity of the teacher. The Bible talks about leaders and asserts a foundational character sketch of persons who excelled, but it does not provide us with the finer points of the leadership process.

Leadership

Too many people attempt leaderlike behaviors without having a fundamental understanding of the process itself. There is no perfect definition for the concept we refer to as leadership. The terms *leader* and *leadership* are often used synonymously, or in the context that leadership is what leaders "do." This confusion is a subtle but common occurrence in much of the leadership literature. Without collaborators, there is no leadership. A definition of leadership that fails to recognize the vital role of participants and that basically suggests that leadership is the sum total of a leader's behaviors is grossly insufficient.

Here is a very workable definition of leadership. **Leadership is a relational process, whereby individuals grant special influence to one or more persons, who in turn catalyze the group to pursue intended changes.** As we break this definition down into its parts, we will better understand the concept.

Relational process: Leadership is a relationship. Some might suggest that you can lead yourself. A person who leads himself or herself is merely one who is self-disciplined and/or self-motivated. Leadership means that people are involved in a relationship of influence. It takes more than one person for a leadership relationship to occur. A person who holds a leader position, but who has no followers in the leadership relationship, is by definition an ineffective leader. The old saying goes, "He who thinks he is leading with no one following, is merely taking a walk." Leadership is more than just a person who is in charge, desiring to make changes. People are a necessary ingredient.

For example, marriage is not a husband. Marriage is not a wife. It is a result of the husband's and wife's relationship with each other. Think of it as a third entity. As a third entity, it must be cultivated and nurtured or else it will die. Leadership is a process unique to itself. It is not the leader. It is not the followers. Leadership is a third entity. It must be cultivated or it will languish and eventually die. Effective leaders know consciously and/or unconsciously how to birth and nourish this third party.

The idea of process means that leadership is dynamic, not static. Leadership is more like a verb than a noun. Influence is always ebbing and flowing. One example of this is in the ever-changing opinion polls on the President of the United States. The savvy leader understands that he or she will forever vacillate in his or her influence. Influence fluctuates due to time and priority commitments, personality differences, emotional states, and any number of other factors. The goal of a leader is to increase one's influence for the benefit of the whole.

Individuals grant special influence to one or more persons: Leaders usually initiate behaviors or fill positions that influence potential followers to become collaborators. But unless a person grants a leader this influence, leadership does not exist. When individuals force influence over others, this is better thought of as coercion and raw power wielding, not true leadership. In reality, the people ultimately possess the power and can diminish the influence of a leader if they choose. History is full of such scenarios.

49

The purpose of granting influence is to allow the leader in turn to empower the group to achieve greater benefits. Thus, leadership is really mutual empowerment. The leader who foolishly believes that his influence does not come from others is very prone to fail due to a lack of humility and an abundance of self-centeredness. Because people who are nonleaders are involved in the leadership process, the term "collaborators" versus "followers" makes more sense. The word *collaborator* implies participation, that the nonleaders are involved in the leadership process. The term *follower* infers a more passive person. The only members in a leadership relationship are leaders and collaborators. Collaborators vary in their individual commitment and influence.

Because we have a God-given right to choose our responses, no one can force us into a leadership relationship. Jesus did not lead in his home community, and therefore he left Nazareth. Scripture says, "He could do no miracles, because of their unbelief." A would-be leader cannot hope to lead when others do not believe in her as a leader. If you do not want to be a part of the leadership relationship, you do not have to be a part. Coercive influence, such as force, blackmail, brainwashing, and similar actions, is not real leadership. For leadership to be authentic, there must be a majority of volunteerism. Pastors cannot assume they are leading just because they occupy a leader position.

Some would like to believe that the only ethical form of leadership is that which allows for collaborators to be persuaded only by their own wishes. That sort of idea is purely fiction. No one lives in a noninfluential world. We are forever being influenced by what people do and do not do. When people propose ethical leadership in terms of free will, they imply the avoidance of manipulation. Manipulation tends to be more of a leader motivation than it is a style of influence. Some of the most manipulative people are those who come across as very loving, giving, and truth-oriented. The result is influencing people to do what is not beneficial to themselves. Persuasion, on the other hand, is basically influencing people to do what is beneficial to themselves. Manipulation seeks to narrow the number of choices for the primary benefit of the leader. Persuasion seeks to narrow the number of choices for the primary benefit of the followers.

Three groups of people exist in terms of leadership. There are leaders. There are collaborators (followers/nonleaders), and nonparticipants. Only the first two groups are involved in the leadership relationship process. Obviously, any number of leadership relationships are going on at any given time. Sometimes, we are the leaders. Often, we are the collaborators. And most often, we are nonparticipants. There are just too many groups, too many good causes, for each of us to be a part of everything.

Each person must select the leadership processes in which he or she wishes to participate. That is why church work can be such a challenge, because sinful people want to avoid God's call, and holy living is not generally our first inclination. Church leadership thus has two challenges, one innately spiritual and the other primarily leadership oriented. Only Spirit-filled, effective leading can overcome these challenges.

By suggesting that a person is a nonparticipant, I do not mean that he or she is not influenced by consequences of the leadership process. The primary objective of leadership is to change things. Where change is not needed, leaders and leadership are not needed. Other relationships can occur such as management, family, friendships, ministry, or whatever brings two or more people together. Leadership is the unique relationship desirable and necessary when intentional change or advancement is needed.

We are all influenced by various results of leadership processes of which we are nonparticipants. One example is policies set by government when we had no vote and even no idea of what was happening. Suddenly we find ourselves paying more for a certain product or tax, or needing to file certain forms. Voluntarily or involuntarily, we chose not to participate in the leadership process, yet we were influenced by the outcomes of the changes that leadership produced. Peripheral members in churches are often nonparticipants in church leadership issues. They may become affected by leadership changes which may serve to alienate or engage them.

Catalyze the group to pursue intended changes: The word *catalyze* is an important one, because in recognizing that leadership is a relationship, it is not assumed that leadership is something leaders do. Rather, a leader is a person who helps make it happen. As a catalyst, a leader will strive to induce the social chemical reaction by initiating action. By casting vision; networking; aligning people; discovering needs, wants, potential, and barriers, and implementing available resources, the leader's responsibility is to get the ball going. Leadership never assumes that the leader will do it all, nor that all depends upon him. As the key influencer, it is the leader's responsibility that leadership takes place. The better the catalyst, the more effective the individual is at leading. The leader must have a mental image of where the organization should go, and at least a beginning idea of how to get there. Without this, a person will not have the potential to bring about change. In rare cases a leader may not be the primary vision-giver, but can facilitate the vision and energy of others to catalyze leadership.

Churches and organizations which do not need to change do not really need a leader. They need good management, a good chaplain, resolution to stay on their course and perform the necessary actions in order to maintain. The changes inferred in this definition of leadership are not so much the many daily changes which occur in a healthy maintenance program, but rather those changes which either affect the core of the organization or which significantly affect the outcome of a certain product or goal.

In the situation where change is not needed, the pastor (leader) would act as a chaplain, public relations person, manager, consultant, preacher, teacher, or whatever other skills the person could bring. In the purest sense, when things are going well, the leader would cease to be a leader and would wear another hat. Organizations only need leadership as changes are desired or needed.

The phrase *pursuit of intended changes* reflects two specific concepts important to this definition. First of all, *intended changes* implies that organizational changes are intentional. By suggesting that churches need to change, the implication is that without change they are staying the same. This is not true. Life is forever changing. Organizations, like people, are forever changing. Unfortunately, when change is not constructive and progressive, it tends to be destructive and/or digressive. Churches, like most organizations, tend to entropy without intentional renewal. There is no such thing as an unchanging church in the truest sense. To stay the same when society and the community changes is to become out of sync with reaching the world effectively. Churches out of touch with the people around them have changed in that they are no longer relevant. Change is inevitable, but growth is intentional. As the old saying goes, "you can't step in the same river twice." Some organizational changes are not good ones and will adversely affect an organization after a time. Intended changes mean that one or more people recognize what is not good, or what can be better.

Pursuit of intended changes also implies that effective leadership can take place without the successful completion of the changes. *Pursuit* means active toward completing, but it does not assume the realization of the intended changes. The process of effective leadership can be taking place ultimately with limited outcomes. There are many causes throughout history that have been led by superior people and that resulted in significant groups of people moving for intended changes, that even so had limited results. At other times we have heralded people as great leaders who did little to catalyze leadership, but were associated with significant change. People who happened along at the right time and place, or as in the church, who see an outpouring of God's blessings, may not be better leaders than those who see lesser results while developing people in leadership. Therefore, it is important not to confuse the health of leadership as a process with the outcome of the process itself. Unfortunately, we have labeled leaders as ineffective because of limited results, while at the same time they were very effective in stimulating leadership. Naturally, a leader who appeared to be effective in leadership processes which consistently did not produce significant changes would be ineffective.

A part of Jesus' messianic ministry involved leadership, namely bringing about spiritual and thus social changes through his leadership groups of the three, the twelve, and the seventy. From all outer appearances, the leadership during his life on earth was only marginally successful when rated in terms of actual output. However, he was very effective in the process. Ultimately that was seen in the long-term effects of his impact through the early church. The rest is history.

Leader

Obviously, leaders play a crucial role in the leadership relationship. The problem is that the word *leader* is used in a number of different ways, many which confuse one's understanding of effective leadership. Three common themes follow.

One definition sees the leader as **a person who is ahead of others,** whether it be in sequence, in prayer, in worship, in sales, or as a pacesetter. We often refer to a company as a leader in a field, suggesting that it is ahead of the others in size, innovation, service, or market share. Such an organization or person may have little to do with leading in the way we are using the term. The leader in a race is ahead of the pack, but rarely involved in leadership. That person has not been given influence resources from the others and is not catalyzing leadership in the pursuit of intentional change. The bottom line is that in a race, the runner is wanting to win, to cross the line before the rest. The first place team or runner is called the leader, even though the goal in competition is generally to defeat the others, not to help them win. Team play and competition rarely go hand in hand.

In a similar sense, we call people leaders if they stand out by demonstrating certain skills such as teaching, prayer, worship, Bible study, or any number of possible behaviors. In the case of a worship leader, small group leader, or prayer leader, the concept of leading is wrapped around a specific role, behavior, and/or skill. For example, a music leader may have few leadership gifts, but a talent in music may determine that person's selection as music leader. This sort of leader influences by modeling, but does not necessarily catalyze leadership in terms of pursuing intentional change. A person can demonstrate a skill and model a behavior without catalyzing leadership. Such a view is a very incomplete leadership relationship. This is not to say that a worship leader, prayer leader, or person filling such a role cannot lead in that role. However, the use of the word *leader* with such an emphasis on modeling or formal initiating as in a service provides a very inadequate picture and really does not help us much in understanding how to be more effective leaders. Therefore, we will not deal with this view any further.

The second most common use of the word *leader* is **the person with the most responsibility in an organization**. A lack of clarity in expectations between the pastor and board often creates tensions. When a board-led church seeks a pastor, they may be looking for a person who will preach, teach, counsel, and manage. If they find someone to fill the position, but the new pastor thinks it is his primary role to lead, to help the congregation make changes, conflict can be expected. This happens occasionally. Conversely, when a church seeks a leader, but the pastor thinks it is his primary role to preach, counsel, and manage, both church and pastor will be frustrated due to conflicting expectations. This happens frequently.

Numerous assumptions are placed upon people who fill roles. The leader is the one with the most responsibility for the health and welfare of an organization. In most churches, the pastor is seen as that leader. When leading is needed, the pastor ought to lead. Even when leading is not needed, the person with the most responsibility is usually still referred to as the leader, even though he may be performing any number of other tasks (for example, public relations, managing, teaching, counseling).

Although a position does not make a leader, the hierarchical orientation of our society recognizes that within organizations we need those who are in charge and who are to be held responsible. For example, a community that needs a teacher will build a school, a classroom, and stock it with desks and teaching aids, hoping to find a person who will fill the role of a teacher. That person may not be a good teacher. She may sit behind the desk and have a name on the door that says "teacher," but good teaching is not guaranteed just because you have filled the position. We do similar things with leaders. We note the need, create a position, locate it at the top, and supply it with resources (plus sometimes quite a few perks) to enable the leader to lead, but this does not guarantee effective leading will transpire. *Leadership Journal,* a fine quarterly publication, is one example of the popular notion that position means leadership. The title would imply that the journal is about leadership, but very few articles focus directly on leading. Most deal with ministerial concerns and church management under the assumption that pastors are leaders by their very position. People typically refer to a person as a leader, based on positional responsibility for organizational health.

If you choose to define a leader in terms of the one most responsible for church health, you would be better off to focus on the effectiveness of a leader to catalyze leadership when it is needed. An effective leader is a person who catalyzes leadership when it is necessary for the benefit of an organization. The leader is effective when he or she is able to respond appropriately when leading is necessary. The leader is ineffective when he or she is unable to appropriately respond to leadership situations where change and organizing are required.

The weakness of a positional definition of a leader is that a pastor may be deemed an effective leader when the organization is going well even though he is really only managing and supervising, not leading. In other words, we often refer to a person as a good leader who may be a good manager or minister at the time, based on the perceived health and stability of the church.

In addition, the person who is actually responsible for the health and welfare of an organization may or may not be the one who fills the official position of leader. Many churches and other groups are really led by those without an official position. That is a difficult thing to understand for many who have the official position. When the person in the leadership position is not the one who actually leads, power struggles and division of churches and organizations will result. In most cases, we assume that the person in the leader position will be the most responsible.

The third use of the word leader tends to be an ideal definition. A leader is **the person or persons with the most influence in a leadership relationship.** This definition is not consistent with positional leading. Position raises expectations of the person in it and often provides some influence resources, but it does not guarantee the ability to catalyze leadership for intentional change. What so many pastors fail to realize is that their position does NOT mean they are the leader as used in this sense. Most of what we are taught assumes that the person holding the position called "pastor" has the most influence or authority in a church. Perhaps that is why seminaries and ministerial training programs do not concern themselves with training in leadership: their graduates will become positioned as pastors and be granted the influence or authority they deserve after studying with scholars in the academy. But reality is that a leader is the one with the most influence with or without any official position. Leaders are those who influence others to change. If you do not have collaborators, then you are not a leader in the literal sense.

We cannot assume that parishioners are collaborators just because they attend our church. A person can have a lot of people in his organization without being a leader. Organizational membership does not guarantee a leadership relationship. The view that a leader is the one with the most influence is the purest definition of the term *leader,* for it places the preponderance of verification on whether or not the person is actually influencing toward intentional changes, not just given the title or position of leader. Although the third definition of a leader is the preferred one in this book, it is important to understand why there is so much difficulty in teaching leadership. One main reason is that the most common definition has to do with organizational responsibility versus real influence. Because this latter definition is not the most common, you will need to translate the concepts of this book into conversations you have when people talk about leaders. A positional leader is often ineffective when it comes to leading because a real leader is determined by the amount of influence he possesses.

Leading

A leader does not "do" leadership. Leading is what leaders do. Leadership is generally a result of effective leading.

We know leadership when we see it, but we have difficulty explaining the process. A definition helps contain a term much like river banks serve to channel water. Even if you do not agree with the definitions as I have described them here, it would be a healthy process to debate them. We often come to terms with our own definitions after we have argued for or against their validity.

CHAPTER 4

EXPLODING
LEADERSHIP MYTHS

B ecause leadership is a social issue, as society changes so does
leadership. The definitions mentioned in chapter 3 tend to reflect
a view of leadership which is emerging as we approach the
twenty-first century. It is a natural evolution seen in civilization and in
how people interact with each other. A major paradigm shift is taking place
in leadership and thereby leadership studies. For the most part, our views
of leadership have been based upon an industrial sort of model, which
tends to be hierarchical, top-down, and centered around the Great Man
theory. The Great Man theory is oriented toward a (white) male-dominated
culture which is more individualistic than team-centered, more autocratic
than empowering. The General Patton, John Wayne "True Grit" sort of
stereotype is still popular among many businesses and churches, although
that sort of charismatic form of leadership is quickly fading.

As society moves from an industrial to a postindustrial era, we are
seeing a new leadership paradigm emerging. This type of leadership is
more team-oriented, more empowering, and less prone to the superstar
(superego) of the past. It is more of a win-win than a win-lose mind-set.
There are several reasons for this shift, but here are a few, briefly
discussed.

The Information Age: The Information Age is only the third era
known to humankind, and it is relatively new. For most of history, the
Agrarian Age dominated as people made their living from tilling the

ground or around farm-oriented careers. Then around the turn of the twentieth century in North America (earlier in western Europe), people began moving to the city and finding employment in the new factories and assembly lines. This was the beginning of the Industrial Age, when a majority of people began making their living by manufacturing goods as society expanded. The Industrial Age ushered in an increased need for management and for a hierarchical style of leadership based on position, rank, and, of course, male domination as most roles were filled by white males. This orientation continued throughout the middle of the century.

In the 1950s, after World War II and with the computer and space age on our doorstep, the Information Age began. Gross national product moved from industry (making things) to the manufacturing and processing of information. The boom of information has made it impossible for any one person to have all the information or the answers. We depend more and more upon others to provide information and specialized insights. This has necessitated more cooperative leadership than the previous autocratic leadership of the Industrial Age. An emphasis on people skills and a less domineering approach to leading began to emerge with the new era.

Enhanced education: With the information boom came an even greater emphasis on education. The depth and breadth of knowledge required more advanced training. The postwar generation became the best educated generation in all history. As education grows, so does the need for more participative leadership. The industrial form of leadership, which is more autocratic and top-down, does not work well with well-trained thinkers. Thus, more democratic and participative styles are emerging that better suit those with more advanced educations. The Great Man theory is based on the idea that only a few people at the top have all the good ideas and know how things are to be done. Education has expanded our awareness for others' ideas and decreased the number of people willing to take orders.

The feminist movement: The feminist movement advanced as women became more involved in business, industry, and the other aspects of society. The baby boomer generation did a lot to advance the voice and mind-set of women. As more women became educated and active in social and business interests, we became more influenced by their thinking. When men built companies, they did it out of a masculine mentality, as a natural expression of how men think and respond. Men and women are different in how they think and relate to others. Women are more relational. They are open more to emotions and passions than merely logic and production. The presence of women in organizations and the feminine influence has done a lot to reshape the concept of leadership, such as enhancing the concern for process versus product alone and developing sensitivity to others as opposed to treating people as a means to an end. Women have taught us to utilize the group, thus strengthening the idea of leadership as a relationship.

Cultural diversification and the global village: Thanks to the information and travel revolutions, we are becoming a global village. Although individual prejudices still exist, people have an awareness of what is going on in other cultures, and there is a sense that we must work together. The ethnic mixing within North America has helped us become more aware of cultural differences. The outcome is that we increasingly realize that our way may not be the only way or the best way, and therefore we need to inquire more, engage in more dialogue, and negotiate. This results in a leadership approach which relies more heavily on give and take and two way communication versus one-way, top-down mandates, quite common in the industrial paradigm.

Democratization: As the walls of Berlin fell, the world as a whole seemed to recognize that communism and dictatorial governments did not work well. The rise of democracy is both national and corporate. People expect to participate more in policies and outcomes which affect them. Therefore, they assume a more participative leadership style. The old school of one or a few people setting policy for the many and telling everyone how they are expected to behave is pretty much becoming a historical way of thinking.

Competition and consumerism: As democracy and capitalism rise and as fierce battles break out to grasp consumers' attention, an orientation toward service correspondingly rises. The business sections of bookstores are booming with books on service. People will move to a vendor who can give them the best service and product. The sheer number of competitors vying for a limited number of clients means that people will not be satisfied with less, and one result is that leadership must become kinder and gentler. Churches that are not able or willing to provide adequate services for attenders are apt to lose them to superministries that do.

People now think in terms of job options, so that they are much less willing to put up with an insensitive leadership style. The days are over when leaders could dictate policy and autocratically give commands because they were confident that they had a corner on the market of the people. A more sensitive form of leadership with an emphasis on relationships and empowerment is emerging out of recognition that if we do not try harder, the clients or employees or collaborators can and will go elsewhere. The lack of organizational loyalty has forced leaders into adopting a style that will cause people to follow out of respect and desire rather than out of subordination and intimidation.

Leadership Myths

Defining leadership builds a base for understanding it. At the same time a foundation is laid, it is at times necessary to tear down existing ideas which deter us from fully recognizing the concept. Here are some of those leadership myths.

Myth: Leadership Is Solely the Leader's Responsibility

If we say a leader is the person most responsible, we realize that a leader is not the only one responsible. The emerging leadership paradigm helps us see leadership as a team effort. The industrial paradigm which is hierarchical, top-down, tends to either idolize or crucify leaders. When leadership is effective, the leader is given an inordinate amount of credit, often coinciding with absurd salaries and benefits. On the other hand, when leadership is ineffective, the leader is often terminated and made to be the scapegoat for the much larger problems plaguing an organization. This is a form of organizational dysfunction and perpetuates a state of denial such that an unhealthy organization will go through a number of potentially good leaders, while failing to see its responsibility for the ineffective leadership. In a marriage relationship there are rarely ever situations where a single person is 100 percent responsible for the health or demise of the marriage. Although "the buck may stop" at the leader, it is rarely the leader's buck alone. Without sharing responsibility, a leader will tend to take on too much guilt and blame when failure occurs and too much credit when success transpires.

One of the reasons we are in our so-called leadership dilemma is that in our lack of community, people do not want to commit. We want the leader to be held responsible so that if things do not turn out as we like, we can blame him. This unwillingness to make a commitment and to bear responsibility is all around us. People blame the government and environment for their crimes committed. Adults blame their parents for their sins instead of owning up to their own decisions. Collaborators blame ineffective leadership on the leader. When an organization fails, the leader is not the only one responsible. Followers are responsible as well.

The Bible says that when one part of the body suffers, the others suffer as well. All the parts of the body have a mutual investment in each other. A leader has the most responsibility. Thus, the leader is more to blame for leadership failure than any given individual, but the sum total of the followers may and often exceeds the responsibility of the leader. Remember that no one becomes a leader without the willingness of others to make or allow that person to be the leader.

Myth: Effective Leadership Equals Success

Try not to equate success with effective leadership. For example, a church in the inner city is trying to change its ministry objectives instead of shutting down. A pastor who is an effective leader comes and provides a vision for growing from 100 to 500 people. Through her vision, people skills, communication gifts, and other leader behaviors, she is able to help catalyze leadership and turn around the church from closing the doors to becoming a vibrant church of 200. Was this effective leadership? The goal of 500 was not met. The objective was not reached. But most of us would agree that this portrayed effective leadership in that the people were invigorated, organized, and motivated, which produced a net increase of 100 in a difficult situation.

Let us take another church, located on the growing edge of a city. The pastor has good ministerial gifts. The church is basically trouble free, maintains ongoing ministry needs to people, and ends up growing from 100 to 500. Can we assume that this pastor has provided effective leadership? Not necessarily. The growth may have had little to do with his leading. It may have had to do with the church location, its ministry management, or the anointing of God's Spirit.

There are many things that can affect outcome. In a political campaign where only one person is elected, it is tempting to believe that the winner is the one who exemplified the best leadership skills. We fail to look at how far the person came, what obstacles were overcome, and how tight and focused the support team was. The runner-up may have actually provided far superior leading; but because of the resources, public opinion, and any number of other factors, he did not outperform the winner in the polls.

If we buy into the idea that effective leadership equals success, we assume that whenever a church or organization has been successful, it is because there was a great man or woman at the top, making it happen. I can think of situations where, through the outpouring of the Holy Spirit, through a certain social movement, or through a crisis, individuals have "found" themselves at the top or in the limelight or as the head of a successful organization with very little effort on their part. When we buy into the belief that leadership begets success, we herald these individuals as great leaders, refusing to believe that they just happened upon the great success. Obviously, success or failure is rarely single-handed, just as marital bliss or dysfunction is not of one mate's making. However, if we are to get a handle on leadership, we need to avoid assuming all credit or blame goes to the individual who fills the role of leader.

At the same time we may herald mediocre leaders as great leaders simply because their organizations have taken off, we can overlook great leaders who are very effective at leading, but whose organizations have not done so well in terms of reaching visible objectives. This is apparent when you get beyond the outer trappings and analyze certain pastors. Some pastors of great churches are more managerial and have a difficult time articulating about leading and organizational growth. Some pastors of "lesser" ministries are more visionary, more articulate and intuitive and are able to show you a well-organized group. Leadership is very complex in that there are so many variables involved. You must look at the resources available such as money, people, facilities, communication channels, and so forth. You must look at the conditions at hand, such as the competition, the timing and readiness, as well as the growth potential. In the church growth movement, we are forever looking at successful models and trying to emulate them, while overlooking the environmental effects of personalities, timing, God, and resources. Then we wonder why it is so difficult to replicate these models elsewhere.

You cannot necessarily judge a person's leadership aptitudes according to organizational size. For example, you cannot suggest that the pastor of a church of 5000 is ten times better as a leader than the pastor of a church of 500, or 100 times better than the pastor of a church of 50. Leadership aptitude is much like the Richter scale in that it often works in logarithmic proportions, that is, a small amount of leader expertise can go a long way. We cannot even assume that the pastor of a church of 5000 is a strong leader. He may be a strong manager and/or have an unusually anointed gift such as preaching which draws the people, while not possessing unusual leadership aptitudes.

Sometimes good leaders are not so much better at influencing others as they are at recognizing ripe situations, organizations that are prime for their gifts and/or ready to "pop," so that their perceived leader skills are also matters of discernment and opportunity selection. This in itself should not be underestimated. In life there are limited time and re-sources. We are constantly prioritizing and making judgments regarding potential payoff and input required. However, to compare outcome without input and potential is to run the risk of misunderstanding leadership.

History is replete with examples of churches growing tremendously under the autocratic and power-wielding tactics of certain pastors. They got the job done. They reached their objectives. But did they lead well? In many cases, no. Staff have been chewed up and spit out. There have been divisions. People have been motivated by intimidation and fear, rather than vision and respect. From all outer appearances, the church has prospered under the direction of a great man, while those more intimate to the situation recognize that it was more secular than sacred, more manipulated than manifested. By developing a mind-set of what leadership is all about, we can learn to look beyond appearances and analyze what aspects of leadership are being done effectively and what are not.

Myth: Everything Rises and Falls on Leadership

One of the first things you learn in logic and debate is that the use of superlatives is impossible to fully support. When you say that "everything" rises and falls on leadership, you have crossed that line. Aside from this more obvious weakness is the concern that those of us who believe in the importance of good leaders and healthy leadership go too far at times by suggesting that leadership is "The" antidote to the world's ills. It is like assuming that if a little cocoa makes a good chocolate cake, then a lot would make a great chocolate cake. This sort of thinking makes for poor judgment in terms of leadership.

The more I study leadership, the more I realize that everything in an organization does not rise and fall on leadership. I believe in strong leaders and effective leadership. However, when you state that everything rises and falls on leadership, you are approaching the idea that leadership is divine.

Leadership is not everything. If you have outstanding leadership but poor management, an organization can fall apart. There are numerous examples of entrepreneurial companies which exemplified brilliant leadership, but which failed due to an inability to provide other facets of a well-run organization.

Leadership is vital, but it cannot be all things to all situations. If you have great leadership, but just cannot obtain the necessary resources, whether they be people resources or material, physical or other, you may not succeed at an objective.

Leadership is vital, but it is not everything. Although the head is vital to the body, the head without a mouth, or a heart, or other key supports cannot function. The head may be the most important single element to the body, but it is not everything. Leadership is perhaps the most important element in the healthy growth and functioning of an organization, but it certainly is not everything.

Os Guinness points out the danger of taking something that works, even a God-given principle like leadership, and making that into our god. The subtle yet strong temptation is to rely on the principle, the tool or technique, more than on God. This goes for positive processes such as marketing the church, electronic evangelism, and all sorts of other techniques that enable the gospel to spread and churches to grow, but which can become substitutes for our faith in believing that God will build God's church.

Those of us who see the importance of effective leadership and therefore believe in effective leading, run the risk of making leadership our god, of depending too much on it and not enough on God's Spirit. Just prior to and since the fall of humankind, we have had the idea that we can control more than we really can. We strive to control our environment, our bodies, people, and organizations. Sometimes we succumb to the god

65

of leadership out of the idea that we can control our organizations and what befalls them. The alternative to "everything rising and falling on leadership" is neither mediocre leading nor passive democratization. Rather, one can adhere to the importance of effective, strong leadership while keeping the balance that everything does not rise and fall on leadership. We realize that even with the best of leaders, there are still going to be problems and at times insurmountable obstacles.

Myth: Influence Is the Same as Leadership

Leadership is an influence relationship. The influence is not only leader to collaborator, but it is also collaborators to leader, and leader to leaders, and collaborators to collaborators. Wise is the leader who understands this complexity of give and take. The old school of thought primarily saw leadership as a top-down, one-way influence, in other words, the leader influences followers. In a leadership relationship, there are varying degrees of influence between certain people and this influence fluctuates. It is dynamic, not static. The goal of the leader is to increase his influence in the leadership relationship, especially among those with more influence.

Leadership influence is different from other types. Just as all fathers are males, but not all males are fathers; leadership is influence, but not all influence is leadership. By suggesting or assuming that influence is leadership, we confuse the concept and make it even more difficult to understand and clarify. There are all sorts of influence relationships, whereas only a number of them are leadership. There are animate and inanimate influencers. The weather, age, technology, clothing, and books are examples of millions of potential inanimate influencers. Relationships imply people relating with each other. If you think about it, every relationship is an influence relationship, whether it be a customer and clerk negotiating a sale, or a mother bathing her children. There is no such thing as a noninfluential relationship. What is the difference between nonleadership influence and leadership influence? By our definition, leadership involves people organized to bring about intended change. Let us look at some ways certain roles influence us.

Inventors and innovators influence by their product development, discoveries, and breakthroughs. This sort of influence need not involve other people and can be as simple as creating a better mouse trap. If the innovator becomes an entrepreneur who develops a corporation around this innovation and in turn hires and develops staff, then the influence would become leadership. The key difference is the involvement and leading of people.

Managers, administrators, and clerks influence us by their ability to maintain systems and how they allot needed resources. We are all influenced by whether we are remunerated on time, or if the bills get paid at work, or if the organization keeps running. However, this influence is not necessarily leadership because change is not necessarily intended and people are not necessarily organized to work toward this mutual change. If the latter does occur, then it is leadership influence.

Ideas and information definitely have the ability to influence, whether in spoken word, print, or video. Most of us have been consciously influenced by teachers and wise people throughout our lives and countless others in subtle ways that are subconscious. However, these people were not necessarily leaders in that they did not rally people together for a unified and mutual goal. If a teacher begins to take the information beyond the classroom and instigates a movement or empowers the students to then implement this information, leadership influence has been utilized.

All of us have been influenced by the lives of parents, siblings, a spouse, significant others, or a mentor. These people often make great influences in our lives as children and as adults. Some of these impacts are destructive. Hopefully, many more are constructive. We are also influenced by our children. The toy corporations recognize this. However, none of this influence is specifically leadership if it does not involve influence for mutual cooperation toward intentional change.

Spiritual influence comes from the Scriptures, spiritual disciplines, and through direct and indirect intervention of the Holy Spirit. This influence is not necessarily leadership per se, and those who are vessels for this sort of influence, such as pastors, need not lead influence us in such a manner. A discipler can have great impact on us without leading.

Myth: Everything a Leader Does Is Leading

As we learn to distinguish between leadership and nonleadership influences, we also learn to discriminate between leadership and nonleadership needs. Leadership tends to be episodic. If a leadership relationship is only necessary when intentional change is needed, then when we are participating in activities which do not directly correlate with this change and/or with the process of change, we are not involved in leadership. A small part of the pastor's work is actually leading. Most of the time she is reading, administrating, doing public relations, counseling, preparing to teach, evangelizing, discipling, modeling, speaking, praying, and so forth. All of these behaviors just listed are not specifically leading. The problem is that when we see people from whom we expect leader behaviors doing these activities, we assume they are leading. Perhaps a part of our leadership dilemma in the church is that we have failed to help people distinguish between leader behaviors and other ministerial functions of a pastor. And every great person is not a leader. Finding a high quality mentor does not guarantee one will learn leadership, unless the mentor is good at leading.

Although leading is only a small part of a pastor's life, it should be a crucial part. Because most churches today expect the pastor to be the leader, pastors who fail to recognize and respond appropriately to leadership situations will be perceived as ineffective and poor leaders. The church and pastor will suffer. The pastor may have a great heart for God and a wonderful skill in imparting the Word. He may have a gift for counseling, a knack for administration, and possess musical and people skills. However, when leader behavior is not exhibited, people become frustrated. The church fails to progress. People will say things like, "Pastor _____ is such a good teacher, but we need him to lead." "We love our pastor, but what we need is someone with vision." Because the pastor assumes that his ministry and management are leading, he will not understand why the people are not responding to his "leading." Commonly, the result is a plateaued or declining church which eventually dismisses its pastor.

Recognizing a Leadership Situation

The ability to distinguish situations requiring leading is often intuitive and becomes an unconscious response in natural leaders, thus making the leadership process even more difficult to communicate. Each chapter in section three depicts a different facet of leadership. Suffice it to say for this small section, a leadership situation has the following attributes.

1. There is a need for significant change in the church/organization. The leader must be able to identify when a change is needed and, if possible, what needs to happen. Statistics can be helpful. Surveys can reveal hidden needs. This is a major part of the vision principle, being able to see what we should be like. In essence, are we moving toward the vision? Is the vision a product or a process? How will we know when we have achieved the vision? What is the difference between where we are now and where we need to be? Leaders stoke the vision. If the leader has no vision, then leader behaviors will not emanate.

If the situation at hand has little to do with this vision, then it does not likely require leadership. It may need good management, counseling, or whatever, but leadership has to do with intentional change items.

2. There is concern from influential collaborators. Just because someone has an opinion about something in the church or organization does not mean that it is a leadership issue. However, when you begin hearing influential people making comments that sound alike, or when they come to you with concerns, that is a sign that leadership is needed. To be effective, a leader must be able to recognize the most influential people in a group and must develop relationships with them. This is why relational skills are so important and where many pastors are ineffective as leaders. Ineffective leaders do not recognize who has influence and often fail to embrace these people either due to wrong priorities, insecurity, or personality differences.

3. A third element in a leadership situation is a problem or action that involves the entire organization. Leaders need to be involved in decisions that will have an impact on all or most of the people. Because a leader carries the most responsibility for the people in an organization, he needs to be present and proactive in events and/or policy that will affect all of the participants. A majority of the meetings and church issues do not affect everyone, but some do. These latter are crucial in terms of responding as a leader versus a minister or manager.

Perhaps the exception to the idea that leading is episodic is when you look at the continual responsibility leaders have to emulate the values and ideals of the organization. This is especially important for a pastor and exactly why integrity and authenticity are critical to pastoral effectiveness. Even though a leader only leads a fraction of her time on the job, she is rarely off duty. The leader is constantly being looked upon as a role model, a public relations person, and in general an ambassador for the organization. This aspect has little to do with leading specifically, but it has a lot to do with perceptions and credibility at key times.

The following chapters will help you further recognize the unique features of leadership so that you can be a more effective leader and/or collaborator.

Part Three
LEADERSHIP PRAXIS

CHAPTER 5

INCARNATIONAL LEADERSHIP

Most of us throw away our broken tools or at least try not to use them. But not God. God's favorite tools are those that have been broken. They may be taped up and nailed together with splints, but they have obviously been broken in the past. This is not to say that God does not use new, unbroken tools. God can bless anyone that God chooses. But God's favorite tools for cultivating and growing his garden are those that have been broken.[1]

God prepares potential leaders by taking them through various character-building events that deepen them in God and purify their motives, dependence, and ego. Scripture says that those in influential roles in the Body will be judged more harshly. Most leaders never imagine the influence they have on lives—until they fail. That is why God is so concerned with developing leaders who are grounded morally, spiritually, and psychologically. There is too much at stake in the Kingdom to be unleashing influence where it can become a dangerous tool for the enemy.

Pastors need to think about how they are leading as well as the character of lay leaders and staff in terms of being broken. Incarnational leadership has to do with leading out of who I am as a leader. It has to do with integrity. The word *integrity* comes from the Latin word meaning whole, complete. Incarnational leaders lead from the heart, not just the head.

Although brokenness and its fruits do not make a person a leader, people who function as leaders without this process in their past should be esteemed lightly in that role. Unbroken people have the propensity to become inconsistent or even dangerous. We have all heard about the tendency of power to corrupt. "What makes the temptation of power so seemingly irresistible? Maybe power offers an easy substitute for the hard task of love. It seems easier to be god than to love God, easier to control people than to love people, easier to own life than to love life. Jesus asks, 'Do you love me?' We ask, 'Can we sit at your right hand and your left hand in your Kingdom?' "[2]

A lack of humility before God is the root of nearly all leadership dilemmas and may be the main reason God chooses not to use many apparently gifted people in leadership functions. Incarnational leadership means one must lead primarily out of who one is, and not what one knows, who one knows, what one can do, or how one can do it. The Bible refers to about 300 people who functioned in various leadership processes. Of these, 100 are listed in more detail, and half of them are listed with enough information that we can basically determine how they finished their careers as leaders. Robert Clinton, a leadership professor at Fuller Seminary and author of *The Making of a Leader* (NavPress, 1988), reports that only about 30 percent of the leaders in the Bible finished well.

The reason leaders fail to finish well is because of inadequate character depth and lack of spiritual dependence on God. Time after time, we see events in the lives of leaders which indicate that God is processing or building the men and women. This pouring of the foundation is crucial for later construction of any sizable structure.

Character to Finish Well

What happens to highly productive leaders who go bad? God seems to bless them, but over time they reveal character flaws. On our farm, we used to build fences. We drove the steel posts in the ground and then stretched wire on them. The posts held up the wire. Sometimes water would erode the soil from the base of a post in a gully. The post would still stand, but now it was held up by the wire. Some great persons begin fervently with God's anointing, but pride and self-sufficiency erode their character. Although they continue in their ministries, the ministries end up supporting them, making them look like they are still empowered by God.

Success and power can be a great leader's downfall. The problem of being fascinated with size and growth rates is that it sets into motion, or at least fans the flames of, our desire for personal success. This in turn tends to promote the unhealthy aspects of competition. I have witnessed several church-growth-oriented pastors touting their church as, "the fastest growing church in _____," "the largest church in the _____." Others do not include numbers, but add that, "I want my church to be the most influential in _____." I could never judge the hearts or motives of these pastors. Only God knows our intentions. I believe for the most part their ministries are anointed. Truly they are flourishing. But statements like these do not reflect an attitude of brokenness.

We run the old Apollos and Paul scenario, in which Paul reminded the followers that he planted, Apollos watered, but God gave the increase. Somehow, we often suggest that formulas, methods, styles, and people give the increase. Humble leaders understand that like the turtle on top of the fence post, they did not get there by themselves.

Leaders easily cast their own golden calf under the good intentions of leading the people in worship. People can be sincerely wrong, and sincerely partially wrong. We run the risk of implying that numerical growth reflects spirituality. We fail to realize that leadership is complex, and so is spirituality. How is it we justify the tremendous growth of some cults and tarnished secular corporations? Or is the church merely another corporation to be run effectively with superior leadership? The copycat mentality is dangerous as we try to clone our styles and our ministries after another who has become so "effective." We deny our unique creativity by trying to "be" just like a more successful endeavor.

A broken person does not care who gets the credit and avoids the implication that the person is responsible for the success. God uses people as he chooses, when he chooses, to the degree he chooses. Our primary goal must not be to manifest results, but to remain available. This is assertive passivity and not an excuse for mediocrity or a "we're not big but we sure are holy" mentality. Brokenness says "I want to be available for whatever God has for me, large or small, popular or unpopular."

Brokenness creates a dependency on God, not upon the needy people who need us. It frees us from the emotional string-pulling that codependent relationships produce. The broken pastor is free to take risks, to model vulnerability, to hold and be held accountable, to confront sin and game-playing with love, and without the fear of losing relationships. Paul says, "Am I now trying to win the approval of men, or of God? Or am I

75

trying to please men? If I were still trying to please men, I would not be a servant of Christ" (Gal. 1:10). It is only when we are free from emotionally depending upon others that we can objectively provide high quality ministry which in turn frees and matures those we shepherd. As leaders, we must be sensitive to people, but not controlled by them as people pleasers, tempted to tickle ears. Brokenness frees us from the strings of popularity and the need to be liked. It liberates us to lead with passion, with the soul of a prophet.

I can use all of the influence resources and leadership techniques available, but when God desires leaders, God desires them to be genuine, developed from the soul outward.

The reason many leaders do not last long and fail to finish well is because the pressures finally get to them. Like cheap chocolate bunnies, they eventually cave in to the pressure because they are hollow.

Churches take on the character of their leaders. Brokenness is the process by which our mixed motivations become purer. The words *humility* and *humus* come from the same root. Humus is dirt mixed with decaying life products. Humility is the fertile soil of the soul, enriched by the death of the old nature. Out of the humus, we grow to be the people we need to become, and we minister out of our overflow. Our ministry emerges from our integrity and our wholeness.

Remembering Who's #1

The world applauds the person who can take control. We handsomely reward those who can control their own bodies (athletes, models), corporations (CEOs, entrepreneurs), information (professors, media), speech (lawyers, politicians), and other people (military, and so forth). May the best controller win. Losing control is negative. "He's out of control" (mad/angry). "She's lost control" (of a class). "Get control of yourself" (self-discipline). "The world is out of control" (chaos, anarchy). But the way of the cross is one of giving up control to God.

Unbroken leadership seeks to take charge. As broken leaders, we recognize that God is in charge. Because I am not in charge, I do not have to worry about manipulating circumstances. James 4:14 reminds us that we "do not even know what will happen tomorrow," in spite of all our plans. We are but "a mist that appears for a little while and then vanishes. Instead, [we] ought to say, 'If it is the Lord's will.'" Matthew 6:25 reminds us that we cannot even add a single hour to our lives, so why worry? Psalm 127:1-2 says that "unless the Lord builds the house, its builders labor in vain. . . . In vain you rise early and stay up late, toiling for food to eat—for he grants sleep to those he loves."

Because I am not in charge, I do not have to fight for my rights. A lot of energy goes into saving face and making sure that justice is carried out on those who betray us. A board member approached me once about someone who was spreading some negative talk about me. He asked, "So what do you intend to do?" I smiled and said, "Probably nothing. God is sovereign." When the Lord is in control, you know that justice will ultimately be served. When leaders fail to heal from past hurts and to forgive those who have betrayed them, they are revealing unsurrendered rights.

If God is in charge, I need to obey his will even when I do not feel like it. The sovereignty of God is not a rationale for lying down and doing nothing. A fatalistic or existential view is not the result of God's sovereignty. Because the Lord is in charge, I have responsibilities, but they are different from the ones when I think I am sovereign. Most important is doing God's will, rather than becoming successful.

Although God would consider faithfulness and success as the same, most of us consider them separately. Brokenness is realizing that the sovereignty of God releases us from the unceasing drive to make things happen, even with our God-given gifts, even for divine service. Great rationalization goes on in the name of ministry when we try to do great things for God instead of striving only to do the perfect will of God. No one is indispensable in Christ's church.

Servant Leadership

A result of being broken in the right place, in the soul, yields a leader with the heart of a servant. Just as leadership is a relationship versus something a leader does, servant leadership is a type of relationship process. It is a relationship whereby a group of people choose to serve each other in unique roles. Servant leadership is about a group of people mutually submitting to each other for the purpose of achieving something they could not achieve alone.

The way one tells a servant leader from a nonservant leader may be different than many people perceive. A servant leader can still be strong, dynamic, animated, and outgoing. During times of intense crisis, a servant leader may be very boisterous and even dramatic. The leader, may be seen with a whip in hand, clearing the temple, or challenging naysayers with their own sins and hypocrisy. We must get beyond the idea that a servant leader is a wimp, someone who really cannot lead dynamically, and therefore backs down to contrary pressures. A nonservant leader may be less outgoing, more docile, and even more sedate. Try to avoid stereotypes and personality idiosyncrasies in understanding servant leading.

What makes a leader a servant leader is not temperament, strength, or energy. What makes a leader a servant leader is first and foremost the type of motivation in the leader. When the motivation of the leader is to unleash the potential of the followers and primarily benefit the needs of the organization, that person is a servant leader. A person who is not a servant leader will tend toward more mixed motives in leading, striving to lead out of pride, manipulation, and force.

Servant leaders understand that means to ends are just as important as ends. A person can feign servanthood by claiming that the goals of the organization are for the benefit of all involved, and that whatever it takes to reach those goals is justified. Each of us know pastors who would claim to be serving the people and would consider themselves servant leaders, but who go about reaching church goals via manipulation, using people, and who privately exemplify a very prideful attitude.

A Servant Versus a Servant Leader

You can be a servant and not a leader. You can be a leader and not a servant. But to be a servant leader, you must first become a servant.[3] A servant leader is one who both serves by leading and leads in such a way as to exemplify a servant's attitude. Two people can do the exact same job, and one be a servant and the other not a servant. A leader ceases to be a servant leader when she ceases to lead with the right attitude. A servant ceases to be a servant leader when he ceases to lead. A leader is one who brings about change via an influence relationship. In the literal sense, a person ceases to be a servant leader when he is not seeking to bring about change.

The typical corporate model in the context of leadership is a pyramid, where managers and leaders occupy the upper domains and the middle managers and laborers inhabit the lower regions of the pyramid. In this model, THE leader is at the top of the mountain where there is greater pay, more benefits, power, esteem, and all the other perks and resources (automobiles, exquisite offices, exclusive dining rooms, and so on) of being top dog.

Quite often, we describe servant leadership by inverting the pyramid, suggesting that in this view the leader is at the bottom, serving the needs of the people. The servant leader has the fewest rights in that the task is to help others find their potential and fulfillment as a part of the organization. I believe this description is very plausible, and I continue to use this as a teaching tool. However, it has limitations and may not be the best reflection of real servant leadership. The reason is that in organizations and churches where servanthood is embraced, the servant leader still receives more perks and benefits than those who are now "higher up." Although inverted from an industrial, corporate model, the inverted pyramid still lends itself to hierarchical thinking.

Perhaps it would be better to think of servant leadership with a model which did not imply higher and lower strata.

| Leader | Collaborators |

Figure 5a. Servant Leader Equality

If we place leaders (see figure 5a) on a single line with others in the leadership relationship, the implication is that there are none higher or lower, but that all are peers in an influence relationship. The amount of one's influence is represented by one's length on the line. The wider the length, the more the influence. People who are not in the leadership relationship are not even on the line. This is perhaps a better view of what the New Testament means when discussing spiritual gifts and the Body of Christ. No part of the body is better than another, just because some are given more prominence. Thus, none are higher or lower, just different. This does not suggest that all are equal in impact. The heart plays a more vital role than the hand. In leadership, the leader fills the key role because without this person or persons the quality of the relationship would be severely reduced. At the same time, the leader is considered a peer, just another part doing her unique job. Because leaders are a minority, they are usually the hardest to replace as well. A linear peer relationship conveys servanthood because it equalizes everyone when the tendency is to elevate leaders, event servant leaders.

Motives are difficult to measure. Perhaps only God can effectively judge such subconscious workings of the mind. However, servant leadership involves a much kinder, gentler approach to leading. It can be equally forceful and dynamic, but does not reduce the self-esteem of followers. Some managers debunk leadership because they have seen so many people get chewed up in the process. They equate strong leading with autocratic, dictatorial, love 'em and leave 'em tactics. This is an indication of ineffective leading and a lack of servant leading. Effective leading rarely leaves bodies strewn along its path due to blowing people over who will not bend to the new goals and vision. Effective leading communicates, motivates, inspires, and wins people's wills. Servant leadership is a win-win proposition. Other types of leading take a win-lose approach, especially if a win-win is not possible or is too expensive. The reason why leadership has at times left bad impressions is almost always due to a lack of servanthood integrated into the process by the leader.

Churches that split over charismatic gifts (such as speaking in tongues), contemporary music, or any number of other reasons are almost always victims of ineffective servant leadership. Godly men and women can ruin churches when they go about transformation through manipulating and forceful approaches. Whether good or bad, those of us who seek to exemplify Jesus' style of leading must necessarily avoid certain approaches of leading. Nonservant leaders may be very successful, but their strategies have no place in God's kingdom. Those who cannot accomplish what they desire through servant leading would do best to improve on their leadership skills or move out of the picture and let someone else rise to the call.

The old sports slogan suggests, "It's not whether you win or lose, but how you play the game." This cliché lacks balance because it suggests that winning is not important. However, we cannot overlook the fact that in the philosophy of Jesus, how you play the game is a part of whether you win or not. Those who lead as nonservants can very well grow the church, build the building, and apparently expand God's kingdom, but they may fail to be successful in Jesus' eyes. Leaders with integrity must be constantly asking the questions, "How am I leading?" "Am I being effective?" "Am I portraying a servant's attitude in the process?"

CHAPTER 6

LEADING THE WAY VERSUS HOLDING THE FORT

Leadership Versus Management

Most churches are overmanaged and underled. The result is religious organizations that function as Christian assemblies, but that lack vision and a proactive energy to seize ministry opportunities as they arise. This does not mean that such assemblies fail to influence their community. Well-managed churches function well until significant changes are required to expand or to fight influences which would cause decline within the organization, such as in an ethnically changing neighborhood or a culture requiring more contemporary means of worship and outreach. Changing times require leadership versus maintenance. Ministry management during a change of environment helps us understand why so many churches have plateaued or are declining (more than 85 percent). So long as there are people to be won, Great Commission work will require advancement, which is generally a leadership domain. Because a majority of pastors function as ministry performers and ministry managers versus leaders, it is important to define both the similarities and differences between leadership and management.

Defining Management

Anyone who has traveled abroad knows the amusing experiences of trying to communicate using words that mean little in the culture you are visiting. Perhaps more interesting are those cultures that are very similar, but that use different words for the same object or concept. For example, in the United States the cover of an engine is called a *hood*, whereas in England it is called a *bonnet*. I was raised calling the evening meal *supper* and noon meal *dinner*, but when I moved to the city and to the West Coast, dinner was always in the evening. In the Midwest you refer to carbonated drinks as *pop* and in the West you call them *sodas* or *Cokes*. Whether it be marriage or teaching or communication of any type, meshing terminology is an ongoing challenge.

A big communication problem when discussing organizations is management versus leadership. Anyone can find brochures, books, and advertisements designed to interest managers in leadership. The assumption is that managers lead. At the same time, we put on management seminars to which we invite church and organizational leaders. The terms *leadership* and *management*, and *leaders* and *managers*, are used so interchangeably that for the most part society assumes these are the same. For the purposes of this book, let me define management and manager.

Management is the process whereby an organization is maintained and inherent structures are perpetuated. A manager is a person whose primary responsibility is to maintain the existing structure of an organization. These definitions are descriptive, not critical. Huge sums of time and effort and resources go into the maintenance and perpetuation of an organization. Our own bodies consume most of their efforts in maintaining and perpetuating themselves to fight disease and death. Effective management is important for organizational health. Anyone who has desired a paycheck from a company, wanted a product on time, and sought longevity for work or service can thank management. There is much to be said about the role of ongoing management which seeks to better itself and find more efficient ways of operating.

Some would imply that when leadership is poor, it is only management, and that when management is good, it is leadership. Good management is not leadership, and bad leadership is not management. A good banana is not an apple, and a bad apple is not a banana. Good leadership is good leadership and bad leadership is bad leadership. We need to keep our terms distinguished.

Management where managing is needed is good. Upon realizing that management is not enough to keep the pace in changing times, people jump on the bandwagon to degrade the important role of managing. A group of people can just as easily fail due to poor management as to poor leadership. They are both necessary and should be done with excellence. In fact, good leaders recognize that good management is necessary and consciously and unconsciously make sure it takes place. An organization can last longer when it is managed versus led, because leading does not focus so much on the infrastructure and care for the maintenance of the systems. However, lasting long is not necessarily the same as being fruitful, effective, and healthy. Many a church and company are enduring a monotonous existence, doing little more than maintaining the engines. Like a boat going in circles with no one at the helm, so is a church or group which is managed but not led.

Conversely, a group which is simply led without the benefit of proper management may take off and soar out of sight, only to crash for lack of organization. It is like a boat with a big engine and a tiny rudder. It is likely to come crashing into a sandbar, a bridge pylon, or over the falls. Any healthy organization, whether religious or other, needs both good leadership and good management to be effective in a changing environment. Well-managed, poorly led groups will likely plateau and keep things as they are. This is all right so long as the internal and external environments do not require significant changes. However, the world we live in today rarely provides for long stretches of such balanced influence. That is why leadership is in more demand, because the environment is changing so quickly.

Although many suggest that management and leadership are basically the same and that we are merely arguing over semantics, a rising number of voices in recent years suggest that management and leadership are nearly opposites. By now you know that I believe these terms are very different, however the obfuscation we find in discussing these terms lies more in their similarities than in their differences.

Leadership and Management Similarities

The main reason why so many confuse the concepts of leadership and management is that they both have to do with supervision. Supervision is the idea of responsibility. Although it tends to be related to a more hierarchical way of thinking, a supervisor is one who is basically accountable for a project or group of people. Supervisors are decision makers.

What determines whether a supervisor (formal or informal) is a leader or not has more to do with the purpose and impact of the decision. Because leaders and managers are supervisors, most assume that their roles are the same.

In his book titled *Leadership*, James Burns popularized two terms of leadership, *transformational* and *transactional*. Transformational leadership has to do with more dynamic, visionary, charismatic changing. Transactional leadership has to do more with political, incremental, negotiated change. While transactional leadership may approach more managerial styles, it is oriented toward leading in that it seeks significant change but through calmer, more negotiated means. Although a lot of politics is merely governmental management, transactional leadership helps describe how leading is typically done in such organizations where sweeping changes are often limited by structure, size, or culture.

In Figure 6a you can see that supervision is basically the family name consisting of overseeing and decision-making activities such as leadership and management. When a supervisor is referred to as a manager and/or a leader, many assume these are the same. I remember coming to a large church which has a number of extended families who attend church together. It took me a while to distinguish brothers from brothers and sisters from sisters because they looked alike. After a while, as I became more familiar with their distinctions, I could name each person individually. As in leading and managing, it is the family resemblance which initially confuses us. They differ primarily in degree of and the process of change involved in the supervision, but they are similar in that one is responsible and "in charge."

Significant Change	Incremental Change	Maintenance
Transformational Leading	Transactional Leading	Managing

Figure 6a. Taxonomy of Supervision

Managing, and its first cousin, administrating, refer primarily to maintenance supervision of organizational structure such as carrying out policy and fiduciary responsibilities. Managing is a sort of link between the product and people, the organizational structure and the services provided. Managing is primarily concerned with the implementation of polity, a process that emphasizes incremental changes to the existing system within the existing environment. Administrating has more to do with resource control such as a comptroller.

Toward the managing section on the continuum, but within the leading parameters would be the aspect of transactional leading. This type of leading emphasizes more of a political, incremental change process. The goal is to initiate significant change through negotiated steps. Transactional leading is less traumatic and perhaps not as deep as transformational leading. This form of leading differentiates from managing in its proactivity and responsiveness to changing conditions in the organization and/or environment.

To the left of transactional leading is transformational leading. This kind of leading is primarily value changing and instills even more significant and penetrating changes. Transactional leading is more evolutionary, yet intentional, whereas transformational leading is more creationist in style. Often, leaders with personal charisma or strong power resources catalyze transformational leadership to take place. These leaders are best suited when significant change is needed right away.

Leadership and Management Differences

Numerous distinctions help the serious supervision student understand whether most functions are leadership or management in orientation. My three boys have distinct personalities even though they have the same mother and father. Although leadership and management are both supervisory in nature, you can see strong distinctions between them once you study them for awhile.

There are three main reasons why pastors manage when they should lead. The first is because natural leaders are a minority. Those who lead naturally, lead with confidence, and lead with an intuitive sense of what ought to happen tend to be few in number. A second reason for a lack of leading is that leading itself goes against human nature. Human nature attracts us to comfort zones, to places of rest and consistency. Leading involves moving people out of comfort zones and creates disruptions, at least initially. Another human nature aspect is self-image. We all want to be liked and accepted. When we take risks and are willing to set a new direction, we are liable to be rejected by some or all. Plus, when you initiate change and new goals, you run the risk of failing at these goals.

Therefore, it is much easier to make few or very minor changes instead of leading. A third reason for the lack of leading when appropriate is because we have not taught pastors to think like leaders. We train them to think like theologians, ministers, and church managers, but few ever receive significant training in leadership alone.

Management is the process of keeping current systems functioning with a primary emphasis on efficiency. Leadership is the process whereby changes are implemented with a primary emphasis on effectiveness. Where these two processes intersect is the place a lot of people get confused. Leadership is a quality of providing vision and detail with concepts, exercising faith, seeking effectiveness, and providing direction while thriving on opportunity. Management involves an authority (based on position) relationship between managers and subordinates for the outcome of product and the selling of goods and services, whereas leadership is an influence relationship between leaders and followers for the purpose of intended changes emerging out of mutual purposes.

The thing that makes management successful is pursuing same-game strategies, things that have worked before. The thing that makes leadership successful is formulating new-game strategies. The organizational goal of management is to perpetuate cultures, whereas leadership is oriented toward creating new cultures. In terms of external/internal change, management strives for stability whereas leadership thrives on crisis. Management tends toward more tangible, short-term results, whereas leadership focuses on intangible, long-term results.

Leader/Manager Differences

A leader is one who helps catalyze leadership. A manager is one who helps catalyze management. Most analysts of leadership versus management suggest that it is very hard to be good at both leading and managing because they tend to utilize different gifts and emotional wiring. An individual most effective in management prefers a structured approach whereas an individual most effective in leadership favors in unstructured approach. "Just as a managerial culture is different from the entrepreneurial culture that develops when leaders appear in organizations, managers and leaders are very different kinds of people. They differ in motivation, personal history, and in how they think and act."[1]

Leaders tend toward self-identity, whereas managers tend toward organizational identity. Leaders question established procedures rather than maintaining existing policies, rely on personal versus positional power, and seek the enjoyment of innovating versus conforming to organizational structure.[2] Managers plan and budget, organize and staff, and control and problem solve. Leaders establish direction, align people, and motivate and inspire. The manager often lacks intuition and sees people as actors in a sequence of events, whereas a leader attempts to see what the events and decisions mean to participants and to work out of vision and intuition.

Perhaps the most cogent explanation of leader/manager differences was published by Zaleznick in *Harvard Business Review*.

"Where managers act to limit choices, leaders work in the opposite direction, to develop fresh approaches to longstanding problems and to open issues for new options. The leader needs to project his ideas into images that excite people, and only then develop choices that give the projected images substance. Consequently, leaders create excitement in work. Leaders work from high-risk positions and are often temperamentally disposed to seek out risk and danger, especially where opportunity and reward appear high. Why one individual seeks risks while another approaches problems conservatively depends more on his or her personality and less on conscious choice. Especially those who become managers, the instinct for survival dominates their need for risk, and their ability to tolerate mundane, practical work assists their survival. The same cannot be said for leaders who sometimes react to mundane work as to an affliction."[3]

"The manager plays for time. Managers seem to recognize that with the passage of time and the delay of major decisions, compromises emerge that take the sting out of win-lose situations. Leaders attract strong feelings of identity and difference, or of love and hate. Human relations in leader-dominated structures often appear turbulent, intense and at times even disorganized."[4]

"Leaders may work in organizations but they never belong to them. Their sense of who they are does not depend upon memberships, work roles, or the social indicators of identity. The methods to bring about change may be technological, political, or ideological, but the object is the same: to profoundly alter human, economic, and political relationships."[5]

The weakness of managerial pastors is to understimulate a congregation that wants to be excited about gaining new frontiers and expanding.

The weakness of leader pastors is that they can overstimulate congregations with their forever expanding borders and campaigns, so that they wear out their people emotionally. That is why it is very common to see a church go from a manager pastor to a leader pastor to a manager pastor to a leader pastor. This is typically done subconsciously, but what the congregation is saying is that the leader wears us out and the manager does not stimulate us enough. What most churches seek is a pastor with the mind of a priest and the soul of a prophet, one who has an attention to church life and ministry but with the passion and vision for reaching their potential. The smart pastor will recognize the need for balance, both in managing and leading well. This means times of risk and expansion when change is needed, followed by a time of maintenance and rest after changes are implemented.

Knowing When to Do What

The challenge of expanding our ministry of leading is in determining what daily activities require leading and what require managing. Differentiating ministry, managing, and leading is at times the most difficult thing to describe because most leaders behave intuitively. Functions cannot always be cleanly dissected. When is my church ready to be led? Better yet, which situations are managerial and which require leadership if I am to be effective as a pastor? The primary difference between ministry and leading is that ministry is an end in itself, whereas leading is a means to an end. The primary difference between managing and leading is that managing has to do with what it takes to sustain and gradually improve ministries and the church, whereas leading has to do with developing new ministries and significantly improving existing church operations. After some thought and practice, a pastor can categorize most of his daily activities. Most pastors would discover very little involvement in leading, either because ministry and managing squeeze out leading, or because they do not know how to lead. Leading is primarily concerned with pursuing positive change by catalyzing people resources.

CHAPTER 7

THE "C" WORDS:
CHANGE AND CONFLICT

L eadership is about change. If you need no change, you need no
leader. In times of change, people seek out more and better
leaders. Therefore, it is imperative that a leader understand some
of the dynamics of change if he is to be effective. Nearly always, change
results in a certain amount of conflict. These two elements are perhaps
the most spurned in many churches and among status quo pastors. Most
people are afraid of change and many pastors are conflict-phobic. Truman
popularized the saying, "If you can't stand the heat, get out of the kitchen."
My philosophy of leaders is, "If you can't create some heat, get out of the
kitchen." Leaders deal with change, and change and conflict go hand in
hand at times.

The Change Myth

Everyone seems to be talking about change. The idea is that if we do
not change, we will soon find ourselves out of touch with a society that we
ought to be reaching for Christ. The title of Leith Anderson's book, *Dying
for Change*, hints at a common myth in terms of change. The title comes
from the obvious perception that a lot of congregations are doing ministry
the way they have always done it. In essence, because churches have not
changed effectively, they are quickly and quietly heading for extinction.
In reality, there is no such thing as an unchanging church.

Early psychology studied people during times of most obvious transitions: they studied childhood, then adolescence; and then they studied gerontology. The underlying assumption was that most adults changed little and therefore did not need to be studied. But when we began studying adults, we discovered that people never stop changing. Adults in their twenties are different than adults in their thirties, forties, and fifties. Life is dynamic.

The same is true of organizations that are little more than corporate reflections of individuals. Organizations change. Because they are a part of their environment, when the environment changes, they change in their relationship to it. What we assume to be a lack of change in churches is really the problem of not making the appropriate changes to have an impact upon society. A congregation effective in the 1950s changed if it did the same thing in the 1990s. It changed in that it was no longer in touch with its community. By staying the same, we often change in our effectiveness and ability to relate, and we gradually decline in energy, productivity, and momentum. That is a grievous kind of change, and the results are scores of dying churches. A church which effectively ministers to its community can stay the same, so long as the environment does not change. When other factors change, the church must change if it is to stay the same in effectively ministering to its community.

Leaders come into the picture when change is needed for the organization to stay the same in terms of matching ministry with community needs. Holding the fort these days will result in impotency and infertility as the congregation ages. Leaders need to be in tune with the congregation and the ministry area so that they can continually catalyze changes which will help the church keep current. If too many changes have elapsed (versus time), it may be too late to bring about sufficient transformation. The only hope is to die with dignity and give birth to new ministries/churches designed to address the new contexts.

Signs That Change Is Needed

Here are five investigative questions designed to analyze if a church needs significant change:

1. Does our congregational makeup match the demographics of our community?

2. What ministries/programs have we seen grow or decline in the last 2 to 5 years? What ministries are over five years old with little change?
3. When was the last time we significantly surveyed our congregation to determine if their needs, hopes, and expectations are being met? (Every 1 to 3 years is crucial.)
4. When people leave the church, what reason do they give? (Or are we even doing exit polling, an extremely valuable resource?)
5. Have I as a leader done everything in my resources to make this church responsive? (If so, it may be time to pray about a miracle or a move.)

Five Signs of Readiness for Change

Addressing the preceding questions can open up discussions as people share observations and thoughts. Often, a result of an honest analysis will produce a sense that something needs to be done. Recognizing a need to change and being ready to change are two different issues. Here are five signs that change is ripe.

1. Is there a strong sense among the most influential people that change is needed? Remember, think in terms of influence. Monitor what everyone says, but pay a lot of attention to those who possess influence in social circles.
2. Do surveys show that the congregation is dissatisfied with the present status? This is not a guarantee, but if a critical mass supports change, chances are it is long overdue.
3. Is there a drastic difference between the "invironment" (internal atmosphere) and the environment? A church that has no hope of expanding its ministry base is on life-support system.
4. Is there a crisis or significant statistical change? This can be one of the easiest ways to bring about change, because people are most willing to follow a leader with a vision when things are obviously not right.
5. Do you have a divine insight that significant change is needed right away? This has to do with vision, one of the most important keys to bring about transformational leadership (see chapter 10).

The difference between the vision and present reality is the amount of change required.

Steps for Implementing Change

1. Know where your people are. If the change needed has significant, widespread support, then you can progress rapidly and with little persuasion. If the change needed has sporadic support, you will meet with specific persons of influence for the purpose of casting vision and building trust. If the change proposed has very little support, then you must take longer and spend a lot of energy in dialogue, gaining interest, and marketing the vision.

2. Create dissatisfaction. People change primarily for two reasons: dissatisfaction with the present and/or a desire for a preferred reality. People who are satisfied in their present state are very reticent to adopt change. A leader typically needs to provide some reasoning and emotion behind why change is needed. Pictures need to be painted. Perceptions need to be corrected. The challenge is to create discomfort without appearing negative or condescending and without appearing to be a troublemaker. Preaching, vision casting, and conversations are ways to sow seeds of dissatisfaction with the status quo.

3. Provide the solution. When there is no perceived need, a solution will not appear welcomed. With appropriate soil preparation, a vision will take root and sprout. When the problem is acknowledged, an answer is more readily adopted. Vision casting can motivate people if it paints a picture of a preferred reality which is greater than a present comfort zone.

4. Organize and plan the change. Fearful people want details. They want to know not only what the changes will look like but how they can come about. Melancholy temperaments yearn for actions and times to be spelled out clearly. A leader with a great vision will often be ineffective if there is not a support system in place explaining how the change can become a reality.

5. Follow-through is vital. A leader is an influencer, but the leader must also provide the goods. Plan your work, and then work your plan. Visionaries can fall flat when there is little to show for the changes after they are adopted. Leaders can gain or lose significant credibility at this point. A lack of follow-through can produce hard feelings and doubts so that proposed changes in the future receive even less support.

Pessimistic Leader's Checklist

There are six popular explanations that pessimistic leaders give for why their people seem to buck change and create conflict.

1. **Human Nature:** People do not like change, therefore they always buck the process.
2. **Stupid/Close-Minded:** These people just are not open to new ideas (usually mine) and they have no clue of what is happening to our church.
3. **Lazy:** These people would rather do anything than make a commitment. They are inherently lazy and want nothing to do with pushing forward.
4. **Stubborn:** This is laziness with an attitude. When I push, they push back. These people are obstinate.
5. **Hostile/Mean:** Some of these people are downright mean. They only appear to be Christians. It seems like whatever I do, some of them are against it and rally others to support them.
6. **Carnal:** The bottom line is sin. If they would give their hearts to God and be filled with the Spirit, things would change around here.

These attitudes coincide with Theory X management, which is generally considered ineffective and limiting, although it is still popularly held today. Theory X managers consider people as basically lazy and unproductive, not desiring to change or improve. No one with a few moments of church experience could deny the reality of items in the pessimistic list above. However, what this list reveals is a trend, an attitude, a disposition that reflects a lack of understanding of organizational change. Leaders who think this way will tend to shut down their creativity and justify their frustration as a leader. Leaders cannot be cynical about people and ministry if they want to be effective. If you think this way, you have two options: to leave or to change your attitude. Changing your attitude will neither guarantee organizational change nor assure you will stay in your pastorate the rest of your life, but it will give you the sanity required to persevere and to find a way to bring about possible change in your church.

Optimistic Leader's Perspectives

Positive leaders project a different view of conflict when regarding change. People who enjoy conflict tend not to be emotionally healthy. At the same time, strong people need not fear conflict. An effective leader realizes that conflict is a natural part of human beings adapting to changes. Spurning it is neither healthy nor does it advance the situation. Conflict leadership has to do with understanding and using the tension which leading creates. An effective leader knows that conflict can represent good signs and can also provide necessary guideposts for a leader to respond appropriately.

Theory Y leaders view people as basically ready to learn and desirous of positive change. Providing an environment for catalyzing this energy is the responsibility of leaders. Here are ten Theory Y perspectives projected by positive leaders who understand organizational change aspects.

1. Remember the law of physics. A body at rest tends to remain at rest. The same is true socially. Generally, the longer a group has been plateaued, the longer it will take to move ahead. People rarely change overnight. Physics shows it takes more energy to move a body at rest than it does to keep it moving. There is a propensity of any group of people to remain as they are. Cursing this resistance is a bit like shaking your fist at gravity.

2. Holding onto the good. Each generation has the idea that its ideology is the best. As leaders who desire change, we tend to believe that change will improve the organization. Before we assume our way is best, we need to see if the people are holding onto current or past structures for good reasons. New is not always better. How can we retain the good of the past while proposing the new?

3. Ignorance. Ignorance is different from stupidity. It means a lack of understanding. Fulfilling the need for information and clarification is a primary task of a leader. Enlightenment is not just something that happens. It needs to be intentional, and many leaders overlook this aspect. We somehow presume that if it is clear to us, it must be clear to everyone else. Detailed, painstaking, methodical explanation and illustration are vital to communicating clearly. Discussion has to be a part of it as well. Lay leaders need to feel ownership, that they understand and see the rationale, before they will buy into a new idea. Many a leader has realized how he jumped to the conclusion that the people were stubborn when they were really just uninformed. An unwillingness to jump to a new vision may be a positive sign of stability, not stubbornness.

4. Familiarity breeds security. Life is complex. In order to reduce the stress of constant change, we tend to select certain tastes, styles, and patterns. Therefore, we are creatures of habit. Something that is familiar, even if it is less than optimum, is usually preferred to an unknown. We all select certain paths to work, friendships, and daily patterns so that we can reduce stress. The known is less stressful than the unknown. Therefore, people are not just antichange because they are sick or mean. It is a survival technique. They seek security. For people to follow a pastor into change, there must be a significant amount of trust.

5. Fear. Although, from appearances, a group may seem stubborn, apathetic, and even hostile toward change, the root of most of these responses is fear. Change means that we are going to have to move from the familiar to the unknown. For example, if new people start coming to this church, I will not know them like I do the present crowd. What if they change the style of worship, or music, or teaching, or we have to build a new building? People are inclined to avoid what induces fear. The chief goal of a leader at this point is to bolster these feelings of insecurity with loads of love and to incrementally build successes so that they feel more confident and courageous to face the unknown.

6. Change often produces pain. Only a masochist enjoys pain. Leaders realize the pain of good change is less over the long haul than the pain of not changing. However, we all tend to have a short-term focus. Change creates dissonance, instability, and a result of this is a certain level of discomfort. Recognize that a reluctance to change is not necessarily a stuck-in-the-rut, rebellious attitude. It may be the honest-to-God human reaction of not wanting to feel pain. New relationships, new buildings, new ministries, and the death of old ones can all produce emotional pain as people are forced to readjust. A leader with a good bedside manner is helpful.

7. Impatience of a leader. Leaders by nature are often impatient. They pursue topics begging for change. A discerning leader will recognize that some of the frustration in slowness toward change is self-inflicted. A leader lacking discernment will tend to project his impatience onto the congregation as slowness and reluctance. Organizations often change slowly on the whole, and impatience can be an asset when used in appropriate doses. Timing (when) and technique (how) are essential change components. Happy is the leader who learns this.

8. People care. Marriage counselors know that the couple that comes in fighting is better off than the husband and wife who have not spoken in so many weeks and couldn't care less about the marriage. Anger and conflict engage people into the process. It signifies that they care about the organization. Leaders often find it easier to turn vocal opponents into allies than nonvocal fence sitters. Passion means energy. The key is turning that energy into constructive versus destructive directions.

9. **Seeing where people stand.** A leader sometimes does not know where the resistance to a project lies until conflict begins. So long as people's thoughts and feelings are hidden, a leader can only guess who he needs to talk to and what he needs to do to bring about the change. During conflict, we can discover who needs more information and what social circles are resistant. Also, a leader learns what aspects of the change create the tension and what issues need to be modified, explained, or dropped. Early conflict can serve as an excellent source to help the leader know how he needs to go about casting vision, what to touch on and what to leave alone.

10. **A certain amount of conflict is good for emotional health.** We all need times to vent. So long as emotional exhaling does not attack people and divide a team, it can be a normal, healthy action. When new ideas are raised, people usually need to process them prior to accepting them. Proposed change elevates new ideas which in turn attracts various opinions. Letting people hear each other during this process can be beneficial and even bonding. A church family that never struggles over issues is not strong. It is a sign of suppressing some heavy-duty problems under the pretense of keeping peace. Congregations need to learn how to cast opinions, disagree, and still remain loving and unified. Do not overlook the potential growth within people during the process, not just as a result of the change completed. The inner growth during times of change is one of the most overlooked benefits of the process. See the potential for enlargement of their hearts, repentance, restitution, and renewal. If we stifle conflict prior to satisfying the emotional need for it, we will likely only postpone and increase the frustration. A confident leader welcomes the conflict so long as it does not tear at people, and he usually gains significant ground in handling it well.

Innovation

People tend to accept change at different rates. You will find that some consistently embrace innovations, whereas others consistently balk at change. A part of this is due to temperament and one's ability to accept adjustments.

Early Innovators	Progressive	Impressionable Middle	Conservative	Ultra Conservative
10%	15%	50%	15%	10%

Figure 7a: Readiness for Change

Early innovators are very quick to adopt change. Many of them easily become bored so that almost anything new seems welcome. Many of these will be the cheerleaders from the very start.

Progressives embrace change readily, but usually after some initial introduction and logical support for change. They want to make sure that the new idea really will enhance the church, but they think in terms of progress. Influencers who are early innovators and progressive are key spokespersons who can help less innovative people feel secure in accepting the change.

A large number can be categorized as the Impressionable Middle. These people require more time and selling to adopt the change. This section is key to establishing a critical mass within the congregation. This represents your largest selling efforts, for as those who are impressionable see the vision and understand the process and benefits, they too will buy into the proposed changes.

The Conservative group are not likely to accept changes readily. They require extra time to process new ideas, and even then may only climb aboard after the changes have been implemented and they see that it is good. Influencers in this group are most apt to be persuaded by friends and family members who have accepted the proposed changes.

The Ultra Conservatives are in nearly every organization in varying numbers. Realize that you cannot base your leading on these people or you will never progress. Quiet Ultras sometimes drift off to other churches, or they grudgingly make the changes externally after mumbling to others. Noisy Ultras can create headaches for leaders. A wise leader will strive not to portray Ultras as enemies, which is what the Early Innovators see them as.

Influencers who are Conservative and Ultra Conservative should be located early and given significant time with other influencers who have adopted the proposed change. Pastors who surround themselves with more conservative peers are less likely to have a reliable pulse of the congregation. They are apt to hold back on changes. Out of fear of losing or offending conservatives, they lose and offend innovators and progressives and ultimately hold back the church as a whole.

Understanding the various groups enables the leader to deal with those who adopt change more slowly. It is best not to rely too heavily on people from either end of the spectrum if you want to know the heart of the organization. People in each of the five categories tend to listen to the influencers who represent their views. By recognizing these influencers, you can invest special time and effort into helping them see the reasons for change and increase your ability to move the groups forward.

Leadership Conflict Skill Highlights

Consensus is wonderful. If you can procure it without compromising on the vision and selling yourself short, go for it. But understand that consensus is not required and may not even be optional when pursuing change. Whenever there is a lack of consensus, expect some sparks. Conflict is inherent with human nature. Here are four important keys regarding conflict that pertains to leading.

1. Know who is involved in the conflict. An effective leader never gets broadsided by a board or congregational vote. Most leading and vision casting is done prior to any vote, so that the exercise is primarily parliamentary. Leaders are constantly getting in touch with influencers and grapevines. If the conflict involves those in the top 10 percent of influence, you are in trouble. If it entails a large number of noninfluential people, do not sweat it. They may need time, but eventually the masses will move in your direction. The key is knowing who is rocking the boat. You cannot always know by votes and board meeting discussions. Some influencers do not speak up. You may need to probe. If you have a number of your leaders who are concerned, this should be a warning sign that you may be going down the wrong road, or that some significant communication needs to take place prior to acting on the changes.

2. Strive not to overreact. Immature leaders have the tendency to overreact at initial conflict which is like adding fuel to a fire. Just as a teenager learns not to oversteer a car with time, leaders learn not to overcompensate when conflict arises. To overreact is to reduce one's credibility and appear defensive and out of control. Confident leaders retain their passion, but they realize that how you deal with conflict can make or break what becomes of it. If the conflict is allowed to divide people and alienate groups, it often diminishes the level of trust in the leader. By dealing with the conflict lovingly but firmly, as if you were expecting it and it is no big surprise, you will generally emerge strong. If the conflict rattles the leader and brings out defensive insecurities, the feel in the leadership group is that the leader may not be trusted to bring about the desired change.

Many dysfunctional people who harbor pools of unresolved anger within them subconsciously search for things to justify their anger. When people or new ideas are elevated, these people will often respond negatively simply because of their injured psyche. They will strive to justify their anger, but the change has little to do with the origination of their anger. People who have been broken in the wrong places become the walking wounded. Walking wounded people can create a lot of frustration for leaders during times of conflict. Understand that these people tend to cause problems wherever they go. It is no accident that they consistently find themselves surrounded by fire. Wise leaders learn to recognize those who require extra grace and strive to create a buffer between the difficult person and leadership roles early so as to avoid conflict down the road. Most discipled lay leaders recognize wounded people within their ranks and can avert significant damage by minimizing the conflict.

3. Increase communication time during conflict. Realize that everyone works on a learning curve. A learning curve requires time to process new ideas and make inner adjustments. Whenever a change is not obviously preferred by people, they generally go through a dialectical process which is both logical and emotional. Statistics, metaphors, affirmations of the past, and an array of messages in varying forms facilitate people in this transition. The bigger the change, the more that information is needed. The more information that is provided, the more time must be allowed to avoid an overload. Some conflict is little more than a request for more information. When people lack clarity, they tend to feel stressed in making decisions. Town forums, coffee chats, pulpit presentations, and audiovisual aids can greatly reduce this stress, thus diminishing fodder for conflict. Communication provides education and persuasion in order to reduce ignorance. If people oppose a change, it should be only after they have all the information.

An exception to this is when change would take place best with limited conversation. Many pastors get themselves in trouble by taking surveys, scheduling endless meetings, and beating an issue to death. Effective leaders possess an intuitive sense regarding to what degree a change needs publicizing and communication. Some issues are best left to handling by core leadership people and the senior pastor. The key is knowing which issues need maximum communication and which do not.

4. Constantly evaluate the cost and benefits of the conflict. Conflict can backfire when it creates more disruption than the change will bring benefit. Conflict tends to reduce the social credits a leader possesses with others, thus lowering his ability to influence. When the conflict gets out of hand or when it creates too much negative energy, a leader might be wise to postpone the change or retreat totally.

Leaders who give witness to the new vision may have to pay a big price. The word in Greek for witness is our word for martyr. Most of us know pastoral martyrs whose visions created such conflict that they had to leave a church. The successors often benefit from such sacrifice, and the church regretfully realizes that the change agent pastor had been right. Many pastors can avoid being sacrificial lambs and eventually enjoy the ranks of heroism if they recognize when to push forward and when to let go. Although it is a worldly metaphor, leading in conflict is a lot like gambling. You must "know when to hold 'em and know when to fold 'em."

The key is to be blameless before God and the church. The history of Israel is full of examples of prophets who were martyred because the crowds and lay leaders did not like what they said. At the same time, milk-toast prophets often compromised on their message in order to save their skin. "Better a live prophet than a dead one," they reasoned. A pastor who has the mind of a priest will recognize the need to create a sense of unity and organizational stability in his church. A pastor with the soul of a prophet recognizes that at times, compromise is worse than not having a church at all. To back down is to disobey God and go against your own heart. Wise, not necessarily happy, is the leader who knows when to push forward and when to let go.

CHAPTER 8

WHAT TURNS ORDINARY PEOPLE INTO LEADERS?

Influence Resources

T he primary factor that turns ordinary people into leaders is leadership influence. Although all influence is not leadership, leadership is definitely influence, and it requires influence to lead. The type of influence a person possesses and uses has a lot to do with how he is perceived. At the same time, how a person is perceived helps determine the extent of his influence as a leader. If you ever met a dynamic leader who did not fit the pattern you thought of in terms of a leader, it is because he or she possessed some other type of influence resources. While natural leaders tend to possess and pursue these almost subconsciously, a person can learn to obtain influence to a certain degree. Influence resources vary in degree, per person and per situation. An influence resource is a form of power that can be used by a leader who seeks to be effective and dynamic. Different leaders use various influence resources.

The Bible describes power frequently, most often the power of God and the Holy Spirit. The most common Greek word for power is also the origin of the word for dynamite and dynamic in our language. Dynamic leaders possess and use power. Power in and of itself is neutral, though some philosophers would dispute that assertion. The word *power* in terms of leadership often conveys a negative connotation because of the misuse of power and power's strong compulsion to test and at times ruin character.

Because of this negative connotation, I prefer to use the phrase "influence resources" instead of "power resources," because influence is the power that leaders use to move people and organizations. Without influence a leader is impotent. In the most basic sense, a powerless leader is an oxymoron. Therefore, it is vital that we understand the different influence resources, and how they can be gained and lost.

Following is a list of the most common influence resources along with a brief description of each one and ideas on increasing them. These are generally explained in the context of your own influence resources, but also think about leaders within your congregation as well. Staff and laity possess varying types of influence resources which can work for or against you, depending on how well you are able to harness this power for the good of the church.

Coercion

Many would suggest that there is no room for coercion as an influence resource in true leadership. Leadership that is pure maintains a voluntary relationship between the leader and follower. The neighborhood bully is an example of one who tries to lead by coercive influence. Coercion is most typically physical power, but can also be psychological and social as well. It is nearly always negative in form. Some would suggest that when a leader utilizes coercive behavior, which is generally physical action or its threat or some other form of punishment, he ceases to be a leader. This is generally true in terms of nearly all leadership activities you and I would face on a regular basis. However, we must realize that this sort of leadership occurs many times throughout biblical passages. In the Old Testament we have prophetic cursing, and oracles that make threats against the nations. We also perceive coercive influence when Jesus cleared the temple courtyards of the money changers. This influence comes by creating fear more than anything else. Coercion is most often a final attempt at bringing about desired change, when other forms of influence fail. Some leaders gain influence when they use coercion against perceived enemies of followers as was the case in World War II.

There are unique situations where this form of influence resource is useful and healthy, but nearly always in drastic situations, such as during times of war, and when a leader or congregation is faced with life and death issues. The person who resorts to coercive tactics must understand that with them come some strong side effects, such as potential mutiny, short-term motivation, and eventual pathological manifestations within followers. Dysfunctional individuals often have coercive people in their pasts.

In recent years, a growing number of people have written about toxic faith, churches which do more harm than good. Generally, this type of church as well as cults are led by people who employ coercion among their influence resources. Our society is less inclined to respond to intimidating and manipulating tactics. An effective leader would resort to this influence in a limited number of situations.

Charisma

The most common influence resource among natural leaders and those who fit the stereotype of a great leader is charisma. The "born leader" is often blessed with an abundance of this personality quality. Like other influence resources, charisma can be used to lead people and catalyze change in groups. *Charisma* comes from the Greek word for grace, and literally means gift. The common meaning refers to one who has personal magnetism, thought to be evidence of one touched by the gods. This influence resource is the most difficult to replicate and understand. Certain people seem to be born with it. Natural leaders often exude this sort of influence so that their mere presence in a room changes the social dynamics. It may or may not be based on looks, height, charm, attire, communication skills, and general poise. Confidence is often a matter of charisma.

Charisma can be relative to certain groups and is not necessarily consistent to all people. This influence resource often overlaps into others. For example, a certain movie star may have charisma with a group of followers such that his opinion on a subject totally foreign to him has influence over others. That is why one needs to be careful when reading endorsements, because when well-known people comment on things outside of their expertise, it is not necessarily good advice. Personality-based charisma can be gained and lost, but usually it is just polished or tarnished.

Both believers and nonbelievers can possess varying degrees of charisma. Some Christian leaders are perceived to have the hand of God on their lives, when really it is merely an abundance of personal charm and well-honed people skills. Or perhaps it is a combination of personal and spiritual charisma, or perhaps merely spiritual charisma.

From a Christian perspective, spiritual charisma can be overlooked as an influence resource that is obtained by the anointing of God's spirit. Some church leaders refer to this as spiritual authority.

Far too much pastoral work is attempted with human skills and even spiritual gifting, without the vibrant power of the Holy Spirit. Spiritual authority is not manmade or temperamental. This kind of influence comes as a result of a man or woman who earnestly seeks God with heart allegiance. Yet, heart allegiance does not guarantee an anointing. Some very fine pastors lack an obvious anointing of God's spirit. Some in the church growth movement insinuate, perhaps like Job's friends, that the larger a church grows the more spiritual is the leader. We should be cautious in assuming that anointed leaders are necessarily more spiritual than those who are not so gifted. Spiritual charisma might be bestowed over the long term, or it might be a temporary accumulation of influence. The gift is most often lost in the life of one who is disobedient to God, becomes arrogant, and fails to trust God wholeheartedly.

One thing we learn about influence resources is that one resource can help a leader rise to prominence, while other forms of influence can keep him there. Many people rise in influence due to an anointing of God, but after losing the anointing, maintain the appearance of God's presence by utilizing other influence resources.

It is naive to think that the only influence in the church is directly of God. Leaders can create change from many influences, but if we are to be God's preferred leader, we must seek to acknowledge God's touch on our lives. Like Jacob, we must wrestle with God until we are blessed. Many of us tire too quickly for that blessing so that our leadership limps along. The people whom God uses greatly for his causes are those whom God blesses with spiritual authority. Prayer, spiritual disciplines, brokenness, and holy obedience are usually prerequisites to this blessing. As Simon the magician discovered, the frustrating thing is that you cannot bargain for or manipulate God's blessing. You can prepare for it and seek it, but for whatever reason, God seems to bless whom God chooses, when God chooses.

Position

"Position influence" underlies authority. Authority is the influence gained by one's role in an organization. You may have heard the saying, "Position does not make a leader. A leader makes the position." This is true in part. However, many positions provide various resources and credibility otherwise not available to a person. A classic example is the office of President of the United States. The reason so many try to get this and similar positions in government is because these people know that with these positions come allotments of power otherwise not available to them. When a man or woman becomes ordained (the position of elder), this title confers a certain degree of influence to the person. When a person is hired as a pastor, the very position has with it some tangible and intangible resources that the wise leader will use to her benefit for the good of others. Typically, position influence is strongest in hierarchical organizations where there are various levels and ranks of people.

Upon understanding this, a leader may want to pursue a certain position or title for the sole benefit of using the influence available to lead. Many times people seek such positions for ego, financial gain, or any number of mixed motives, but we must not piously dismiss the potential for good in such positions just because people misuse the resources with mixed motives. The CEO of a company can do a lot more to lead and bring about change than can a division manager. The senior pastor of a church has the ability to catalyze a church to greater extent than can an associate or staff member, namely because of the position. Gaining the position does not guarantee the person leadership aptitude, nor does it mean that other influence resources are not needed in addition to make leadership effective. It does mean that in certain organizations, position influence is significant—if you want to get things done.

Expert

Expert influence is based on one's ability to succeed at a task. The task may be a specific skill or a general ability gained from experience or talent. Expertise tends to be specific to various situations. For example, if a group of people need someone to lead them out of financial disaster, they would probably look to someone who had practical knowledge in the area of finances or fiscal recovery. This resource may last only as long as the expertise is needed. Pastors possess varying degrees of influence resources in areas having to do with ministry, preaching, organizational management, and so on. They often lack credibility when it comes to business functions, such as marketing, unless they have proved themselves in these areas.

Interestingly, the roles of character and integrity fall into this category for pastors. If a pastor is unable to satisfactorily practice what he preaches, he is considered incompetent and usually released from ministry. The more the pastor models spiritual maturity, the more credible he is considered and the more enabled to influence. Spirituality and the fruit of the Spirit are often overlooked as influence enhancers by pastors who would be leaders.

Competency is a crucial ingredient to overall credibility. Attend any seminar and you will find that generally the most influential person is the expert. The reason is that the people attending the seminar are seeking solutions, ideas, and understanding. Many pastors find themselves out of work after their competencies are used up and/or after the congregation discovers they are incompetent. A leader must surround himself with new ideas, skills, and approaches in the area in which he works. Incompetency, a lack of expertise, is a quick way to lose leadership ability because it is related to influence. In the context of a local church, the greater the people perceive the pastor to be an expert, the greater will be his ability to bring about change in that organization. That is typically why larger ministries seek out those who have shown competencies in past and present ministry settings.

Effective communication is crucial for productive leading. Expert communicators are almost always in demand as they are perceived to be more knowledgeable, able, and competent. Furthermore spiritual gifts, when combined with expertise are crucial for the Christian. God grants all believers certain expertise so that they are able to be more effective than others in those areas of service to the Body of Christ. Developing your gifts and playing off your strengths tend to be more beneficial than spending the bulk of your time working on your weaknesses. Leaders are generally able to excel in a few areas and thus influence others. In order to bolster their weaknesses, effective leaders surround themselves with experts, so that they can make the most of the resources of these people as well.

One of the most common errors of pastors is in trying to handle things such as financial planning, marketing, and the like, when board members and lay leaders have more expertise. After running multimillion dollar companies, many business professionals find themselves attending a church board meeting, listening to a pastor struggle over minute details of church operations. This is a sure way to lose credibility in the eyes of collaborators. Know your strengths and maximize those while building a team around your weaknesses. This enhances your expertise influence.

Information

Expertise generally involves the effective application of certain information. However, information in and of itself is power, now more than ever, which means that appropriate information is power. Just because you know a lot about something does not mean you will have influence. If the information is needed for the situation, you become influential. Naturally, this and other influence resources can be used for manipulation and destructive measures. Blackmail and "insider trading" (eavesdropping to gain advantage over others in the church) are examples of this sort of information use.

Leaders are readers. They are forever striving to learn and keep up on new information. Books, fax data, cassettes, the Internet, book reviews and condensed material, advanced degrees, articles, journals, videos, and seminars are all avenues for gaining information influence. Living in the Information Age provides a host of possibilities with computer networking, teleconferencing, and a plethora of information materials. However, information for its own sake quickly leads to overload and does not necessarily result in the ability to influence others. Pastors who are peering into their computers as a hobby, and who are surfing the Internet instead of seeing people, are flirting with an information addiction that can remove them from influence among a worshiping community. High quality information is key with the growing number of info vendors. As the Information Age progresses, the best informed will be perceived as the most worthy to lead because of this influence resource.

In addition to formal information lines, effective leaders are also tuned into organizational grapevines. Many pastors have been blindsided because they were unaware of views dispersed among parishioners. Others have been misled by listening to the wrong people who have communicated inaccurate or incomplete information. The wise leader always has an ear to various circles of influence in his or her organization in order to not under- and overreact to important information.

Reward

Reward refers to one's ability to satisfy certain needs or desires of others. For example, a person who can give raises or make large donations has influence merely by this ability. This sort of influence resource can come from having positional power, referral power, and monetary power. Leaders need to understand these influences when working with others. Reward influence involves both a leader's ability to reward collaborators as well as a leader's ability to be close to those who can reward a person or project.

Some pastors are intimidated by people in their congregation who have much money with an ability to reward. Although we might not think of money and financial resources as a reward, this fact of life often works comparably to other rewards in the secular domains. Every pastor knows that wealthy people tend to get more attention than normal because of their funds, especially if a building needs repair or replacement, but it is also dangerous for a pastor who wants to be a leader to avoid people because of their ability to reward (that is, subsidize) a certain ministry. A leader is much like the owner/general manager of a factory. The general manager must take a hard look at all of her assets. A leader must consider his people assets. Are they talented, wealthy, good-hearted but under-resourced, too busy or unavailable? A wise leader builds bridges with those who have the ability to influence for the purpose of including them in the leadership process.

God forbid that we prefer the wealthy over the needy or that we relate to rich people merely for their money. This is more of a heart issue than a leadership matter. However, if a person has resources and the ability to reward a person or project, a good leader must consider this a part of the whole equation and build relational bridges. Money cannot buy everything, but it erects buildings and hires staff so that the many are benefited by the few who are generous and able.

Some pastors alienate high influence people in churches due to their own insecurities, ignorance, or their unwillingness to understand the leadership process. The result of this is that they have occasionally lost the people who wanted to be a part of the vision, or they have lost the rewards of the people because they did not include them in the leadership process. James warns us not to favor those with money with special seating. The context for James's message is not so much favoring the rich as individuals, as it is favoring them and simultaneously overlooking the poor. Do not overlook those who have reward influence in your church. Do what is necessary to build bridges, and harness their energy and interests for the benefit of the kingdom of God.

A church has some great rewards to give if we are able to effectively convey the importance of the eternal and in finding fulfillment by helping others. The lay ministry movement is a great example of a critical mass of people in society looking for significance outside of their jobs and in addition to their recreational lives. Now as much as ever, people are looking for things to invest in which are bigger than themselves, which help others, and which have some enduring meaning. We have the opportunity of rewarding people with ministry roles which can bring this sort of fulfillment. A wise pastor unleashes people appropriately and thus rewards them. Subsequent notes, appreciation banquets, and inclusion of persons in the dreaming process are significant rewards available but often overlooked by nonprofit leaders. You can reward people with a new title, an expanded ministry, funds, and networking. Different people desire different rewards for motivation. Knowing what makes various people tick greatly improves one's influence ability.

Referent

Expertise influence refers to what you can do. Information influence refers to what you know. Referent influence refers to who you know. The person who has a big telephone index, or a sizable phone database, and plenty of "cards to call" is able to go a long way with this influence. More and more, it is who you know, and not what you know that makes a big difference in life. This influence resource relies on one's ability to make phones calls and ask favors and to meet with others who are able to get things done via their own influence resources.

Far too many church leaders underestimate the importance of this resource because they "don't like politics." Politics, simply put, is about building relationships. We almost always rely on established relationships of trust to get something done. We tend to utilize these more than expertise and information, which is why so often the known person gets the job over the more qualified individual. Call it politics or whatever you want, it is about knowing people and establishing friendships.

I have heard many war stories of pastors who needed a favor in the community, whether it be from city hall, a local politician, a builder, or banker. Unfortunately, the leader had not taken the time to get involved in their worlds, rubbing elbows with them at socials, and basically developing relationships. Most pastors do not personally know the local politicians, and then they wonder why it is that the governing bodies will not give them the zone change or permission to expand, which they seek. Or they wonder why they feel like a stranger when the community is in need of their leadership during a social crisis.

Leaders should be writing notes, having lunches, and doing what is necessary to continuously expand their social networks. In recent years these kinds of strategic alliances have overcome the stigmatized "good ol' boy" network (which often kept others out of decision-making, unless they belonged to the right country club or lodge, or had the appropriate skin color) so that church leaders can do business with those who have established some credibility and trust along the way. A wise church leader will not only constantly nurture and expand her relationship with influencers in the church, but will also network those with referent resources outside of the church as well. Knowing people who know people extends the influence beyond one's immediate sphere of influence.

Influence resources are not in and of themselves good or evil. We need to see these as important parts of leadership effectiveness. The person who wants to lead but who pretends to avoid these issues is only handicapping himself and ultimately the organization he is trying to lead. Effective leaders not only strive to utilize their own influence resources but learn to see these resources in others and then enlist them as needed. Too many pastors are intimidated by lay people who have various influence resources and either ignore these lay people or actually end up alienating them. The best approach is to love and disciple these people so that they not only give allegiance to God, but also avail themselves to you and the church.

Like it or not, these influence resources are key to understanding the ability leaders have to catalyze leadership. Without them, leadership does not happen. A leader can intentionally strive to gain influence in situations and must strive to keep from losing it if he or she is to serve effectively as a leader. This has nothing to do with the individual worth or character of a leader as a person. Influence has everything to do with a person as a leader.

CHAPTER 9

DEVELOPING PEOPLE POWER

The People Business

Leaders are in the people business. As I talk with lay leaders and denominational officials regarding what they see lacking in pastors, the most dominant response is people skills. People skills have to do with how a person interacts with others. The fact that you aced homiletics, Hebrew, systematic theology, and graduated summa cum laude from seminary is no indication of how well you work with people. The greatest asset of any organization, especially the church, is its people. Knowing who you have on board and how to relate to them has everything to do with where you go and at what speed. Effective leaders understand how people think, feel, act and react, and are able to communicate interpersonally. All the while, they keep their eyes fixed on the vision and on the subsequent goals paramount to the organization's effectiveness. Balancing these two are quintessential for the successful leader.

Tasks Versus Relationships

By nature, many leaders are very task oriented. They have an agenda, and they want to accomplish it. This task orientation creates the change mind-set of setting goals, developing an organization, and accomplishing the objective. Leadership is basically a process whereby people accomplish things together as a team. The problem is that a high task orientation often sees people as means to an end. Task-oriented extroverts are seen as uncaring, manipulative, and autocratic. Task-oriented introverts are seen as uncaring, aloof, and managerial. Naturally, a leader who is not perceived as caring will develop difficulties because people are the major components in fulfilling the task. Individuals who are strongly task oriented might do better working alone, or as part of a larger organization, fulfilling specific tasks which do not require strong people skills. Task-oriented people who are motivated are often high achievers. They get the job done. By achieving they are often elevated to positions and roles of supervision. But they also go through staff, and eat up good people with their accomplishments, because their task becomes the primary purpose. In a society which rewards the achiever, many of these leaders rise to the top regardless of the hard feelings and tattered egos that they leave behind.

We might assume that the best persons to lead are the relational persons. These individuals are intuitively aware of those around them. They want to build trust with people, create social circles, and strive to meet needs and strengthen relationships. The people person thrives on communicating, on being sensitive to others' needs and feelings and on being available. In meetings, the main agenda is enhancing friendships. Tasks come second.

The problem with leaders who are predominantly relational is that they will often expend their energy toward people versus tasks, resulting in a strong group of people accomplishing too little. Extroverted relational people like to have fun and reach out to people (sell, evangelize). Introverted relational people enjoy simple fellowship and spending time together (counsel, disciple). Leading, however, sometimes means stirring the pot and pushing people out of their comfort zones. Leading nearly always includes conflict, accountability, and at times confrontation. These elements make the people-oriented persons uncomfortable, so that they succumb to others; and instead of rocking the boat and accomplishing the task, they make peace and love people.

In most situations the best leaders are able to naturally or intentionally maintain some sort of balance between being people oriented and task oriented. The result of this balance is an ability to work well with people while maintaining a keen sense of direction and accomplishment. Going too far in either direction limits a leader's ability to bring about long-term change.

Being a People Person

People skills come more naturally for some people than others. There are introverts and extroverts, serious leaders and humorous leaders, but the bottom line is that a leader needs well-honed people skills. Some of this comes naturally. There are many books on understanding various temperaments and dispositions. Recognizing the different ways people think and process information is vital to social effectiveness. If you treat all people alike, you will alienate yourself. Whether it is with the help of Emily Post, Dale Carnegie, or Toastmasters, intentionally develop your people skills. Seek out a person who is gifted with people and ask him or her to mentor you. One of the best ways is to ask your peers, supervisor, and congregation to critique you from time to time. Good questionnaires are available which allow people to do this in the context of leadership, off the record so they can be open and honest (e.g., see *Leadership Behavior Analysis II* by Blanchard Training and Development, Inc., Escondido, California. Or the book, *Listening and Caring Skills in Ministry*, by John Savage [Abingdon Press, 1995] contains numerous exercises for sharpening these skills among church leaders). We rarely see ourselves as others see us. People skills will allow us the best potential for developing a positive emotional bank account with others, which is imperative in long-term leadership relationships.

Social Banking

Leadership is a social relationship. It is never done privately but involves people working with people for team results and organizational accomplishments. In a relationship, each member has an account in the other person's emotional bank. Whenever good things happen because of you, you are making a deposit into your account in that other person's bank. This deposit may be due to providing employment, fulfillment, ministry, a paycheck, self-esteem, or organizational significance and recognition. Credits may come from time, friendship, trust, love, and nurturing of some sort. A leader understands that he must be in the continual process of being sure that deposits are entered into the other person's bank. When you have built enough of a balance, you can begin making withdrawals.

A withdrawal is basically an expectation, something you request or demand of the other person. When you ask your secretary to run an errand for you, or call a meeting during an evening, or delegate a ministry task to someone, these are all withdrawals. On a macroscale, when a pastor casts a vision for a new building and then asks the congregation to give sacrificially, or when a new program is suggested that would change what has been done over the years, these are larger scale withdrawals. If withdrawals exceed deposits, the account is frozen and a leader will not be able to get anything else from the people.

Social banking works the same in marriage, friendships, and pretty much any relationship. If one individual makes too many withdrawals, the other person will eventually stop responding. An exception is when there are outside rewards that the person might be receiving adjunct to the immediate relationship (i.e., serving God by giving). This helps us understand why some marriages seem to suddenly screech to a halt. Over the years the husband has been making withdrawals from the wife, expectations such as preparing meals, washing clothes, rearing kids, and cleaning the house. The wife rarely complains and says little. Suddenly she is threatening divorce or worse, packs her bags and leaves. The bewildered husband stands dumbfounded in the empty home. "What did I do? I never beat her. I provided a good income." The problem is that he had maintained a negative emotional cash-flow for such a long time that bankruptcy finally resulted.

In a church context, people will often go to great lengths to please a pastor and participate in a new dream. This commitment continues as long as there are either enough reserves in savings or enough credits flowing in to cover the amount of withdrawal.

Effective leaders consciously and subconsciously consider three things in motivating people.

1. What will it take to motivate these people? There is no such thing as an unmotivated person. Leaders must help people find in the goal what motivates them. No one factor moves everyone. Browbeating is no replacement for elevating what it is that makes this vision worthwhile.

2. If I do not have what it takes to motivate them, how can I get them to value what it is they can get from participating in this

experience/cause? The Sermon on the Mount is about helping trade earthly values for heavenly. A part of the leader's work is to help people desire what it is they or the vision have to offer. History shows people will transcend Maslow's hierarchy of needs to pursue more lofty priorities.

3. Am I as a leader sufficiently providing for these rewards in order to keep the people motivated? Is the leader providing more positive than negative experiences? In other words, after the withdrawals is there a positive balance?

Social Audits

A leader needs to be constantly taking social audits of both paid and lay staff. Auditing could be as blatant as a church vote or a survey, but is usually informal and often nonverbal. Periodically check in with the top influencers in the church. When they become drained, weary in well-doing, and poured out, they will eventually pull back from your leading and the leadership process. Listen to the grapevine. Sense the energy in a worship service. An alert leader always has his ear to the ground to determine how the people are feeling.

In new relationships, people will often give you a line of credit. This is a grace period based on your perceived credibility, your reputation which precedes you, or simply because they believe in the cause and its potential. This grace period allows you to make requests and demands from them, even before you have had a chance to prove yourself and make actual deposits. The psychological idea is one of investing, hoping that people's investment will pay off over time.

When a person is unproved or has proved ineffective in the past, there may be no grace period and the leader must right away invest time in making deposits. An example of such a situation would be when a pastor has had a failure of some sort and then must make amends prior to making requests of others. Another example would be a church that has had a terrible distrust for its leadership, so the new pastor must spend time loving the people and gaining their trust prior to making any changes or expectations of them. Pastors who are naïve to this social bank account often come into a new situation, make demands of people, and wonder why the people are not more motivated. Pastors often end up criticizing laity privately or publicly from the pulpit, when their own ignorance caused the lay inactivity.

Generally, a leader will need to store up a certain amount of social credits prior to suggesting changes which usually cost, at least during initial periods of visioning and implementation.

Although many pastors fail to understand this social bank account concept and overdraw too early in their pastorate, many more pastors fail to understand when and where the congregation wants change and therefore fail to build up social credits by catalyzing change in the right areas. When laity are looking for a leader, when they are searching for someone who will bring about change, whether it be in a specific ministry or for an overarching vision for the church, their pastor had better start implementing some changes right away. A pastor who implements few changes because he thinks he must earn credits over time loses influence when the congregation is counting on changes. It can take time to build up social credits in credibility and trust, but time can also work against a potential leader who does not recognize the hopes and readiness among the people. Many pastors lose credibility in the eyes of the congregation because they are reticent to implement changes and are seen as either fearful, incompetent, or lacking discernment as to the congregation's needs. This is why many congregations seek leader pastors after extended times with managerial pastors.

Although the stories of resistant congregations abound among ministerial grapevines, I am convinced that there are more laity desirous for change than there are pastors to catalyze change. The problem more often is that the type, manner, degree, or speed of change suggested by the laity and the pastor are incongruent. Therefore, you have a pastor who sits in his study day after day, muttering under his breath about the lack of vision among the laity, while the laity are having roast preacher every Sunday because they perceive him to be a small thinker, void of leadership competence. This dynamic tension happens a lot more than we would like to think.

The primary responsibility of the pastor, filling the designated role of authority in the church, is to find out what it is the laity desire to do and then to expand and mesh that with his own sense of vision for the church. Discovery can be facilitated in board retreats, leadership brainstorming sessions, and staff/board workshops with an outside consultant. All of these can produce significant social deposits in the pastor's account with the congregation if they perceive him as leading the way and staring down some tough future decisions that need to be made. When pastors come in like milk toast while the leaders of the church are looking for change and direction, they hamstring their ministries because they fail to respond to the expectations and hopes of the laity. Therefore, a pastor must quickly get in tune with the intentions of the church leadership (versus the congregation as a whole), to see how far and how fast he should start. Too much or too little can significantly reduce the social bank account of any leader who desires to bring about change within a church.

People Quotients

Since people are the most important asset of every church, a leader's primary job is to maximize the innate potential in the group as a whole. We keep searching for the perfect parishioner in hopes of cloning DNA samples. No church has ever had perfect collaborators, just as no congregation has had a perfect pastor. Effective leaders know how to best use existing strengths to develop the optimum team. In order to do that, they must continually assess those who possess leader abilities as well as those who are able and willing to participate in the leadership process. All people are not the same. Some who are really talented, exceptional individuals are poor collaborators. They do not want to participate. Others with marginal strengths prove to be wonderful leadership participants. Every pastor knows what it is like to have the wrong person in a certain ministry or leader position, resulting in mutual frustration and a dysfunctional program. Ineffective pastors tend to fill ministry holes with living bodies, providing the perception of ministry. Leaders strive to marry strengths with needs.

Testing researchers have determined that instead of having a single intelligence quotient (IQ), there are really five areas of IQ: language skills, science, arts, athletics, and social skills. Typical IQ tests given in schools only measure the first two, and thus are not necessarily reliable predictors of performance or perseverance toward advanced accomplishments. As pastors think in terms of people within congregations, they often try to analyze individuals according to a single factor or category, whether it be spiritual gifts, church experience, education, or professional career. Effective leaders recognize at least five different quotients in determining what people resources exist in a congregation. Applying the five quotients to specific people should provide a better understanding of why certain people do or do not perform to your hopes.

IQ (intelligence quotient): This refers to the basic concept for which it is known. Sometimes those of us in the spiritual world underestimate or downplay the role of intelligence. Perhaps in God's economy, this may be the least important of the five quotients, but as a leader you need to have a feel for the intellectual abilities of your people. Try not to confuse intelligence with formal degrees. There are many "smart" people without college diplomas. Intelligence refers to one's ability to conceptualize and think. This quotient helps determine the speed a person can pick up a goal or objective and handle complex situations. A person with a lower IQ will often not be able to handle situations or projects which demand a lot. On the other hand, those with higher IQs are more apt to be potential leaders, for a leader needs to be able to process a lot of information, to see the big picture, and to coordinate an endeavor. IQs tend to change little, so try hard not to give tasks that are too simplistic to high IQ people, or tasks that are too difficult to those with lower IQs. Love them all the same, but utilize them appropriately.

AQ (attitude quotient): AQ is nearly always more important than IQ, especially in the realm of the church. You want a team of positive people. How do you find high AQ people? Look for people who have gone through some challenging circumstances and yet have a positive disposition. There are plenty of talented, intelligent people who are cynics, skeptics, who will do very little to help you with your congregation's mission. Attitudes are often more reflective of self-esteem. High esteem people have positive outlooks. Low esteem people usually struggle with seeing what is good and hopeful. A negative person (low AQ) can undermine the best of causes if allowed a significant role.

You do not want staff or church leaders with low AQ, even if they possess vast church experience, talents, and skills. The goal is to try to find minor ministry roles for such people and to strive to find high AQ people for positions that will build enthusiasm and momentum in others. Attitudes tend to be infectious, good or bad. Low AQ people are limited in what they can ultimately produce, for so much ministry is a matter of faith, hope, and love—and all of these are reflected in our attitudes.

SQ (spirituality quotient): Spiritual maturity and vibrancy are obviously important in the church. A common temptation for pastors looking for talented, willing people is to make judgments on outer appearances and then turn unqualified people loose in church ministry. The bottom line is that unless a person has a certain level of spiritual maturity, that person cannot perform effectively for long in a spiritual role.

One mistake I made early in my church-planting experience was placing a man who was a bright, successful businessperson on our supervision board. As a church planter, I merely wanted anyone who could help us get going. This man turned out to be pretty young in the faith, and he eventually left the church because I had placed too much responsibility on him too fast. The Scripture says that leaders should not be new believers (1 Tim. 3:6).

Make sure you get to know a person for a while, watching how he or she performs in various less-influential ministry roles. Those who have high SQs will tend to respond like servants and blossom. The low SQs tend to want their names in the bulletins and are likely to fail if the task requires a heart for God. There are various ministry roles available for those with low SQ where spiritual depth is not necessary. You do not have to be a Christian to pass out a bulletin, but you certainly better be a person of prayer, Bible study, and preferably a tither to be on the church board.

A very important ministry for effective leaders is identifying those with leadership gifts who are spiritually deficient. Personally disciple these people in the faith and work with them. These people will serve as a vital leader pool as they mature and become churchmen and churchwomen.

RQ (resource quotient): Resource quotient is a bit of a catch-all in that there are all sorts of resources. Usually, resources fall into three categories: time, treasure, and talent. High RQ people are nice to have on your team, but their resources tend to be only available as their AQ and SQ increase. We all know people with really high RQs who do little for the church and practically nothing for God.

We had a man in our church with a high RQ based on available time. He took early retirement from an aerospace company and became my assistant, a full-time volunteer administrator. We need to be constantly aware of those with time resources and plug them in. On the other hand, the most talented and earnest people are not good team players if they are never available. In essence, they have a low RQ, at least in this aspect. Senior citizens, homemakers, and successful businesspeople are often high RQ people regarding time.

Another family in our church had a high RQ financially. A leader must look at this RQ when going into a building campaign as we did. If you have a church full of people with good hearts and great attitudes but who have few finances, this will greatly affect the outcome of your leadership objectives.

A third category is talent. This talent may be spiritual giftedness, skills, expertise, education, leadership abilities, or even certain networks. People with high RQs in this area are often very tempting for us in that we think of what could be done through them. However, resources are merely tools. The motives and availability to use these tools are the keys to making such people a part of a good leadership process.

As a church/organization grows, those with lower RQs often become displaced by those with higher RQs, creating a tension at times and a feeling of being unwanted. A good leader first looks out for the health of the larger group, but sensitively responds to the lower RQ person, expressing thanks and trying to find another ministry with less demands. For example, as our church grew, we stopped asking certain people to sing specials because their talent did not fit the quality we needed, even though they were willing to provide it. Sometimes people will understand. Sometimes they will need to find another ministry or church which is looking for such a person.

MQ (motivation quotient): There is one more quotient not represented by the others. Pastors have seen people with high IQs who did not add much to leadership. Church leaders have seen those with high AQs you enjoyed being around and who were positive, but who never followed through on a task. We each know of several persons who are high SQs, who love God and know scriptures, but are not influential in our church. You can think of quite a few with high RQs, who do not act on that strength. A crucial quotient is MQ, the motivation quotient. This quotient consists of a combination of temperament, personal energy, and zeal for a church or organization. The Bible calls it endurance or perseverance (Romans 5:3-5). High MQ people are those who want to jump in and get involved. They want to commit, to see things happen, to do something. They are people of passion.

We all dream of high MQ people. Jesus' disciples were high MQ people, especially Peter. Like Jesus, from time to time we have to pull back on the reigns when high MQ people run over others or fail to see the big picture. High MQ people emerge as they mature spiritually and as your leading provides excitement, vision, and meaning. All of this results in momentum. When momentum is low, you can have all the other quotients high, but your leadership team will go nowhere. MQ is not necessarily the most important quotient, but it is vital to getting things done. The best-intentioned people in the world will never have an impact for Christ unless they are moved and willing to commit to seeing a cause or project to completion.

There is no secret formula for these quotients. Leaders think in terms of what people do and do not bring to the leadership process. We make leadership mistakes when we place high quotient people in certain roles when their abilities may not warrant it. We make wrong assumptions and end up either being disappointed in them and/or they become disillusioned. Everyone has strengths and weaknesses. We want to play off our strengths while working on our weaknesses. You may want to even go down the roster of your staff/members/attenders and give ratings according to these five quotients. (Do not share these ratings with anyone.) Then consider how they might best function to create more effective leadership. Effective leaders are those who are best able to maximize the strength of the group by best utilizing the quotients of the individuals.

Detecting Potential Leaders

Developing ministers adds to your ministry. Developing leaders multiplies your ministry. Leaders need to be about detecting, developing, and unleashing other leaders. A skill much rarer than leading well is the ability to discern early on who has leadership aptitudes. Many leaders who lack discernment recruit or hire those without leadership abilities. Although you do not need to be a leader to recognize leaders, effective leaders learn to look for and see those with leadership aptitudes. Some people are born to lead, and other leaders are born out of unique life experiences. Regardless, they are a minority and must be sought intentionally.

As a pastor, I am looking for lay people with leadership aptitudes who will be able to supervise ministry. Too often we select the best-hearted people with a passion for a certain ministry to lead it, and then we wonder why more people do not get involved and why the project never gets off the ground. I am convinced that in developing ministries, we will not plan an event, program, or ministry when a person with leader gifts is not available. If it is a vital program and no leader is found, then I will do it. We need to let a lot of our good ideas just lie fallow until we find leaders. The old saying is true, "Leaders are like eagles. They don't flock. You find them one at a time."

Detecting potential leaders is not a science. However, there are signs of those who might be worth your efforts in leadership training. Four main keys help you discern those with potential leader gifts.

1. History: Look for those who have effectively led some type of group in the past. A brief interview can pick up signs of leadership aptitude. Listen to hear if the person was the student body or fraternity president, or the captain on the basketball team, or simply perceived as a student leader while growing up. Past leading on the job, on the school board, or as district supervisor are strong indicators of leader gifts. Multiple leader roles is almost a guarantee that a person has some degree of leader aptitudes. Society has a way of detecting those with leadership aptitudes, thus allowing you the opportunity to take advantage of what others have uncovered. Sometimes those with leadership gifts do not volunteer for leader roles because they see the pastor leading or the pastor does not want to share leadership. At other times they are weary, do not want to appear presumptuous, or merely need some motivation.

2. Presently leading in the marketplace: Many church attenders are never tapped for their leader potential because the pastor does not know what they actually do at work. Investigate which people are leading in roles outside of the church. Just because a person fills a certain position does not mean he or she is a leader. For example, many people who are managers are not leaders. Some people may own their own business but do not oversee employees, meaning they have trade skills but not necessarily a leadership aptitude. Leadership work usually means they are responsible for a certain number of people and organizationally they help change things versus primarily maintaining activities that others lead. If a person is presently a leader at work or in social circles, the chances are high that he or she might become a leader in the church.

One major precaution is important at this point: DO NOT suppose that marketplace leaders should directly become church leaders. Church leaders need vital spiritual prerequisites that many other leaders do not have. A lot of Christians assume that because they lead elsewhere, they should lead in the church. A leader with differing core beliefs than an organization will usually be a detriment if given a chance. Character qualities such as a godly lifestyle, being a good role model in and out of the church, and spiritual maturity are all crucial fruit for church leaders.

3. Spiritual gifts: A healthy church body will be able to recognize those with leader gifts. They will tend to elect and nominate those whom they respect as leaders. The healthier the body and the more spiritual gifts are taught, the better the group is at discriminating good leaders from good people. Many Christians are nominated for leader roles on the mere basis that they are well known and very dedicated Christians. Activity is not the same as giftedness.

One time I took our board through the confidential process of listing the most influential people in our church. We had grown to the point that I was not able to provide personal care to all people equally, so as a leader I needed to invest most of my time among the top influencers who would in turn be empowered to minister to the others. I asked the question, "Who are the most influential 20 people in this church?" (You could pick larger numbers if desired.) With a flip chart handy, I wrote names and we voted on how many approved of the nomination. It was amazing how well we agreed on the list. Occasionally, a person appeared on the list who did not have leader gifts, but who was visible and active. This allowed me an opportunity to explain the difference between a person who is very involved in activities and is spiritual and the person who has natural influence abilities. A dedicated nonleader may be more influential than a nondedicated leader, but the chance of long-term group effectiveness with this person will not be high. After some training, the Body of Christ will learn to distinguish those with leader gifts and will tend to elevate them to their appropriate roles.

One way to go about helping people determine who the leaders are is by asking questions such as:

"If they left, whose absence would cause several to ask 'where is . . . ?'"

"Who tend to make an impact on several other people when they give their opinion?"

"Who has a following of others in the church?"

"Whom do others seek out when they are looking for a perspective?"

The answers to these questions are not necessarily those people with money, position, longevity, commitment, or an outspoken manner. Influence can be quiet and occasional and yet strongly sensed.

4. Testing: A fourth way of uncovering leadership aptitudes is through diagnostic tests. Spiritual gifts tests are a start. Other instruments include DISC, Myers-Briggs, and a battery of other available questionnaires. Every instrument measures different personality features, but those listed can provide some feedback as to temperaments that are more inclined to catalyze change in groups. For example, those who test higher in dominance and intuition on the DISC test will tend to have greater inclinations toward making change a reality. They will be less inclined to be conformists and to allow things to stay as they are.

These instruments help us uncover some of the emotional/social wiring in people. Since leading is primarily a social skill set, it is important to possess a disposition that allows one at times to buck the status quo as well as to get others to join . These mind-sets and comfort zones help us predict those who are most apt to feel comfortable bringing about change within a group of people. Predicting is different from determining. Possessing a certain temperament does not determine leader success just as a lack of the right disposition does not determine failure. Sometimes we try to assume leader attitudes in those who are not inclined to help induce change but who are willing to buck status quo. When we do this, everyone becomes frustrated.

Qualifying Leaders

What do you do once you discover someone with leadership gifts? The fault of many churches is that we make it too difficult to become a member and too easy to become a leader. Although local church membership was not discussed in Scripture because the early church was just getting organized at the time of Scripture's completion, biblical support for church membership is basically a personal acknowledgment of knowing Christ and a desire to identify with a local congregation. In my own denomination, we have rather high expectations of people prior to becoming a member of a congregation. However, once a person becomes a member, he or she can be elected to leading posts. The Bible says that there are more stringent qualities expected of those in influential roles than the rest of the body (Titus, 1 Timothy).

When you find that a person is a leader, consider this person for discipleship and spiritual mentoring. If you get your influential people focused on God and full of God's Spirit, you will take care of 90 percent of your potential church problems. Foolish leaders do not realize this; and because they do not know the influencers are intimidated by them, they do not win them over and ground them in the faith. There is nothing worse than a carnal person of influence when you are trying to do the work of the Lord. Sometimes it is not even so much a matter of carnality as it is an issue of helping the person understand and support the vision of the church.

Invest regular, quality time in relationships with current and latent leaders. Move toward spending a majority of your time in leader development. Minister to your leaders and to their families. Develop friendships. Share your vision often. Brainstorm with them. Disciple them in the faith so they are biblically and doctrinally stable. Mentor them to be quality churchmen and churchwomen. Build up your social bank account. This is your most significant congregation for the purpose of increasing the quality and quantity of your overall ministry.

"But what if people get jealous and say it isn't fair?" Chances are, they will. Life is not fair. Imagine a team that is playing for the basketball championship. The score is tied with ten seconds left on the clock and a time out is called. One of the players from the bench walks up to the huddle and says, "Coach, I haven't gotten to play in the game yet." The coach says, "You know, you're right. That isn't fair. Let's put you in the game and let you have the final shot." No coach in his right mind is going to do that. The goal is to win the game.

Too often, out of a desire to be fair and to be liked, we compromise our best talent for those who just want to be involved. Jesus did not treat his disciples the same. He spent more time with the twelve than the seventy and the masses. Of the twelve, three were in his inner circle. Of the three, one was known as his favorite. The parable of the talents confirms that all people are not created equally. Ineffective pastors are so concerned with being accused of playing favoritism and with what whiners will say that they leave their best assets undeveloped. Love everyone, but discover those with the most influence and invest your very best time in helping them carry on the vision. Effective leaders know that is the best thing they can do for the betterment of everyone.

CHAPTER 10

VISION CASTING VERSUS GOAL SETTING

The Power of Vision

"Where there is no vision, the people perish" (Prov. 29:18 KJV). Another translation says, "The people languish for lack of vision." If you want to see where you are going, you need good vision. Any organization must have vision if it is to continue healthy and well, especially in times of transition. Churches that wander around in a fog do so because the leader has failed to develop a clear picture of where they are headed. When Jesus talked about the blind leading the blind, he may well have been referring to leaders, spiritual or other, who have no inner eyesight as to where they should be headed.

A vision is a mental picture of a future reality. A leader sees a new sanctuary when it is little more than a vacant lot. The leader can describe the new church plant when there is nothing more than six people huddled in the pastor's living room. A leader will be able to describe the growing, thriving church when it has been plateaued for the last decade. Vision is a future reality that creates present hope and direction.

Although reductionistic, the primary difference between a leader and a manager/minister is probably that of vision. Leaders are constantly associated with, driven by, and talking about a vision. Countless pastors wonder why it is that so few people follow their suggestions, but they rarely think about the role of vision in the leadership process. I believe it is the single most important element differentiating a leader from a nonleader. This is where the soul of prophet comes into play. Prophets often foretold what God intended to do. They painted pictures of prosperity and abundance, or chaos and suffering. Their vivid talk provided mental pictures of what the future would look like, given certain actions and attitudes. Over the last few years, a growing number of writers have focused on this aspect of vision, and yet no one has come up with a magical way of producing it. It is so challenging to communicate a vision because it is almost always intuitive (understood by the right side of the brain) and emotional. The visioning process is truly the most difficult concept to explain, much like trying to describe the grandeur of the Grand Canyon to a person who has never been there. Some authors have tried to actually teach the vision into an organization, but I do not believe you can teach it.

You can strive to explain and emphasize the importance of a vision, but obtaining one is intensely personal and acutely mystical. This mystical receptivity is why those of us who have visions for spiritual growth, and who ponder the supernatural, ought to lead the way in explaining when (and barely how) a vision is produced. Certainly not all visions come from God; but being oriented toward faith and the unexplainable mysteries of God, we make room in our paradigms for that which is mystical and spirit induced. Robert Schuller said, "Anyone can count the seeds in an apple, but only God can count the apples in a seed."

Management Versus Leadership

Management theory is not in the vision business. Managers deal with goals, strategic plans, and objectives; but leaders deal in visions. A vision is the mother of goals. A goal without a vision often wanders aimlessly, lacking motivation and a point of view. You can have a goal without vision, but you cannot have an effective vision without finally depicting goals and strategies. Goals are logical. Visions often transcend logic. Visions move and inspire us. Managers look at their budgets and plan appropriately. Leaders look toward God's resources and ask, "What is it you want us to do here?" Budgeting is always a secondary issue. The "how" never precedes the "what" in visionary leadership. Money and resources flow to visions, not the other way around. The concept behind managing is control. Vision takes risks.

Vision is about Promised Land living, fighting giants, and pioneering the unknown. Joshua and Caleb were visionary. They said, "Let's go for it!" Managers tend to hold back and fear the unknown, often wandering in the wilderness. Managing is necessary in order to hold the fort; but when it comes to entering Promised Lands, leading is required. Managers justify their recommendations. "There are indeed giants in the land." Managers can always tell you rationally and logically why their ideas are the best, but in God's work, risk and adventure often transcend the safe and sound.

When Peter Wagner studied growing churches, he found common spiritual gifts in all of the pastors. The common threads were not as one might guess: not preaching, pastoring, evangelism, or administration. The common threads were faith and leadership. We are all called to believe, to express faith; but the spiritual gift of faith is the ability to trust God for what is beyond the norm. Faith is the "substance of things hoped for, the evidence of things not seen." First Corinthians 13 says that the three enduring themes of life are faith, hope, and love. Love is hoping in others and having faith in them. Hope is faith in a future reality. Faith is hoping for what is not yet seen. A vision is something you intensely long for that in turn produces great hope, a key element in leadership. A vision is future oriented. It is always on the horizon. Once you have something, you no longer hope for it. Ironically, the downfall of many leaders is the completion of the vision. Not long after the completion, hope is greatly reduced until another vision is in place to pursue. A pregnant woman knows this feeling after the birth of her child, and many graduate students have sensed it upon completing an advanced degree.

The difference between an inventor and a leader is that a leader involves other people in the dream. A leader is a social artist, an organizational inventor. A corporate vision is an idea, a dream, a burning passion for something that involves other people. The primary difference between those who would merely manage and those who would lead a local congregation is vision. Time after time I meet pastors who are intensely frustrated with the lack of responsiveness in the people and the apparent apathy within their churches, but they cannot clearly articulate a vision for the church themselves. What every pastor must realize is that if she intends to lead, she must parent a vision. Babies do not just happen. If they are to be healthy, they must be fed, attended, changed, washed, nurtured, and cuddled. A vision is no different. It must be conceived, birthed, cultivated, polished, discussed, and promoted.

Too many pastors are like the boy who went to the wood stove and said, "As soon as you start putting out some heat, I'm going to put in a log." Stoves do not work that way. If you want to get heat, you have to put in some wood. A vision is the kindling by which you light a fire in the hearts of your people.

A church mission and a church vision are different. Mission tends to be more biblically generic, such as worship, evangelism, fellowship, and discipleship. Mission statements tend to be hard to measure and heavy laden with jargon and theological slogans. Vision is more specific as to how the mission will be carried out and what it will look like in the context of this local church. God is not redundant. God gives each body a distinct plan in a community. Every church should have a mission statement, a succinct one sentence purpose and value statement. However, a good mission statement is not the key to growth or enduring change. Many churches have lofty mission statements, but they lack vision in their ministry.

Is it necessary to have a vision in order to be a pastor? If you merely want to pastor, to shepherd, to feed, and nurture your flock, you do not need a vision. A mission statement will do. This distinction derives from the same situation we described at the beginning regarding pastoral roles. If you and your congregation are not looking for a leader in a pastor, but rather more of a spiritual technician, a vision is not very important. Assume the role of a priest, and perform your duties with excellence.

If you want to be both pastor and leader, then you must pursue a clear, compellng vision for your church. The prophetic pastor exudes a sense of destiny, a "this is why we're here" clarification of activity. Most natural leaders are never without a vision for very long. The average American pastor moves every three to four years, hardly long enough time to develop and pursue a vision. Perhaps the main reason for so many transitions in the congregation is that pastors are not doing what is necessary to establish a vision for the church. The cookbook approaches tried during brief pastorates are meager attempts to meet an intuitive need. Such an approach is like reading a pamphlet to prepare for childbirth.

Initiating a Vision

Visions come much easier for some people than others. Perhaps this is a result of spiritual gifts, such as faith or discernment. It may be in part a by-product of creative aptitude and right-brain orientation. It usually exudes from a temperament willing to risk and disrupt the status quo. Effective leaders initiate, cast, and plan to implement a vision.

How is a vision born? We hope, because our work is in the church and ordained by God, the vision originates from God. Thus the spiritual leader will opt to fast, pray, and seek God's strategic will regarding the ministry and mystery to which he is called. This is based on the theological assumption that God still communicates with his people, and especially those leaders who seek God by interjecting thoughts, ideas, and spirit-filled dreams which fulfill the phrase, "thy will be done, on earth as it is in heaven. . . . " Isaiah 42:9 says, "See, the former things have taken place, and new things I declare; before they spring into being I announce them to you." God announces plans to leaders before they spring into being. This is called a vision, a mental picture of an intended reality.

Some qualified managerial pastors strive to reproduce a vision by surveying people about their reactions to a slogan, or by facilitating study groups. With all due respect to participatory leadership, vision is not a result of committee work or small group reaction to a brief statement. You do not expect to vote on it, like you do a budget, a board member, or some other project. Surveys, study groups, and committee work are primarily for the purpose of vision casting and implementation. A leader is wise to get a pulse of the people early, to see how the vision might be cast and fleshed out. But if you are looking for consensus, if you are waiting for some burning theme to emerge or reinact from a group of people, you will be disappointed by the concept of vision. Managers are consensus takers. Leaders are consensus makers.

In the narratives of the Bible vision is predominantly an individual responsibility. Abram had the God-given dream of establishing a holy nation. Joseph had a dream of preserving Egypt and his family from a famine. Moses had a dream of freeing the people from slavery. Joshua had a dream of leading the people into the Promised Land. Nehemiah had a dream of rebuilding the walls of Jerusalem. David had a dream of building a beautiful temple for God. Peter had a dream of what the early church might be like. Paul had a dream of expanding the church beyond the Jewish nation.

India did not gain its independence from England single-handedly, but it started with an individual named Mahatma Gandhi. Germany attempted to rule the world through the leadership of an individual, Adolf Hitler. Chrysler was flailing until Lee Iacocca cast the vision. God used

John Wesley to dream the dream of a revived England through spiritual renewal. The Promise Keepers movement which began in the 1990s was not the result of a committee who spawned the idea for a series of men's rallies and a gigantic movement. It was one man, Bill McCartney, who shared with his friend that he had a vision to fill a stadium full of men, committed to taking a stand for God in their lives.

The possible stories are endless. The point is that vision is not initially a group process. It starts in the mind and heart of an individual. Groups do not have children. Women have children as individuals. Yet, the world is populated. Groups do not start visions. Leaders give birth to them, one by one.

We have all sensed when reading a book or listening to a speaker, that the communicator was saying exactly what we were thinking. A leader is like that. He or she is able to put into words, create a plan, and provide a structure whereby people affirm, "That's what I've been thinking we should do. I want to be a part of that!" Perhaps the thing that establishes some people as leaders is the simple principle of being able to crystallize ideas, helping them seem coherent and plausible. If others do not affirm that the leader's dream is theirs as well, it is doubtful that leadership will happen effectively.

Many managers confuse the idea of participatory leadership with relegating the responsibility of initiating and casting vision in a quasi-democratic fashion. Participatory leadership means the leader does not dream his dreams in a vacuum, aloof from the needs and views of the people. It means that leaders gather opinions and listen to people in the midst of prayer and dreaming. Surveys may be taken for the purpose of knowing how receptive people are to a vision and to what extent it must be cast. Participatory leadership means you include key leaders and activists in strategizing, planning, and polishing the vision for ownership and refinement, but the onus of responsibility and origination comes from God through the leader.

A few leaders are able to carry out someone else's vision without it passionately becoming their own. Only rarely are great things accomplished when the pastor is not visionary. Sometimes, strong lay leaders carry the vision, which the pastor supports but does not initiate or cast. A few times, the Holy Spirit has worked in such a strong and spontaneous manner that both pastor and people basically watched God's vision come to fruition. But most of the time, God uses individual pastors to convey God's dreams for the congregation.

Visions have life spans. They may last for short or long periods, extending well beyond the life span of an individual. When one vision ends or when God is done with you in his vision, it is time to discover what the next vision is all about. God prepares certain people for certain ministries at certain times. If you do not believe this, you will have a more difficult time discerning what vision you ought to be pursuing. You cannot effectively do another person's vision. The copycat mentality has killed a lot of well-meant imitations. All too often when God blesses one person or one organization, others flock to see how in the world they did it. They did not do it in the world, which is why all attempts to replicate the results are ultimately futile. We can learn from others, but it is best to learn how others grasped their vision so that we can do the same with our own vision.

If you do not have a specific vision for your life and/or ministry and you want to be a leader, intentionally seek God for a clear direction. Pray, fast, take a sabbatical, and seek the Lord in solitude. Jesus constantly did this during his ministry. Once you grasp a vision, goals, strategies, and tactics all tend to come in line more naturally. Although a person does not need God to have a personal vision for an endeavor, pastors serve at the will and call of God. We therefore do not have the option of pursuing our own visions and dreams. Let God show you what he has in store for you, and like Jacob, do not stop wrestling with him until he has blessed you with it. You may end up with a limp, but you will also become the parent of a great people. No one can show you what your vision is. No one can give you their vision if you are to be a leader. Seek God and bathe your vision in prayer to be sure it is indeed of God.

Casting the Vision

The place for surveys, board discussions, and committee work has more to do with vision casting than it does with vision producing. The idea is not so much that the leader comes up with the vision and then forces it on the people; rather, the people must be able to participate in the process of ownership. Knowing God, the people, and God's plan for them, the leader starts sharing this. If the vision calls for significant change, then a leader would be wise to share it in bite-sized chunks rather than dumping the whole load on an unsuspecting audience. It may come by way of snippets in newsletters, sermon illustrations, or small group meetings where the pastor can share his heart and allow for a sense of emotional security and dialogue. The main difference between a dreamer and a visionary leader is that the latter knows how to communicate his dream so that others want to enlist.

A wise leader knows how far away the people are from catching the vision. The closer and more ready the people are for change, and specifically the change implied by the vision, the more quickly the leader can share the whole picture. The further the people are from grasping the vision, the more groundwork needs to be covered to help them see the need, see what it could become, and then see how it can become. The bottom line is that a leader must know his or her people. A leader need not be so concerned about the people as a whole as much as the influencers. If the influencers catch the vision, a leader can progress quickly. If the influencers need time to process the ideas and see how they can benefit the group, invest the time with them. Brainstorm and dream together.

Whatever you do, do not wait for total consensus before you launch forward; otherwise you will never get anywhere. There should be a bit of fear and trepidation if a vision is one of faith. An obvious, "no brainer" vision probably does not have much of God in it. As a pastor, make use of preaching and teaching times to cast vision. Show from Scripture what it means to trust God and to dare for the seemingly impossible. Make a point of talking about the vision in your writing, newsletters, and in small group discussions. Put on a special banquet. Print T-shirts, coffee mugs, buttons, banners, special logos, and talk it up. The more you can hint at and openly talk about it, the more the people will take ownership. Visions are like colds; they are caught. The infectious leader has the ability of passing the vision virus.

Ownership is the key word and goal of vision casting. Visions that die are visions owned by the leader alone or by those who are not the influencers. A sure way to kill a vision is to delegate it to one with little influence. It is not owned until people have in their minds a fair facsimile of what is in your mind. Realize that these pictures will not be identical, though we are looking for a basic picture.

Leaders get in the most trouble when they do a poor job of casting the vision. When dreams die and organizations fail, it is almost always because the leader ineffectively communicated what it is she saw as the future of the group. That is why communication skills are so vital for the pastor who would be a strong leader. The ability to motivate and speak publicly are desirable but not essential. Many strong leaders appear rather timid and docile, but no one doubts their passion and confidence in the vision. Whether outgoing or not, they must be able to persuade. You need not be a great orator to convince people, but you must be committed to the vision yourself. If you cannot muster enough sincere enthusiasm for the vision, then do not count on someone else to run with it.

Implementing the Vision

Leaders who merely dream dreams and cast visions are eventually labeled as hot air bags and charlatans if they are not able to eventually harness the dreams to reality. After a few years these people are pegged as being all talk and little action. Cheerleaders and motivators appear to make great leaders, but they leave little in terms of leadership legacy due to a lack of implementation.

I have seen several examples of people who exuded a strong sense of enthusiasm, charisma, and a go-getter' attitude, but who found themselves trying to do everything alone. People will stop and listen to a person who dreams a dream and points in a direction, but the real key to leadership is whether this person is able to get others organized and on board to make the dream a reality. Sometimes perceived leaders are little more than geysers, Pied Pipers of temporary zeal who lack the capabilities and/or skills to see the dream to fruition. A leader must persuade but a salesman is not necessarily a leader. Leaders must motivate, but motivators can be lean on leadership aptitudes. Some temperaments are better at casting vision while others are better at implementation, but both are very necessary for leadership effectiveness.

A vision that has no structure tends to evaporate quickly. Significant visions require sacrifice, and this challenge must be invoked when the going gets tough and when problems arise as they always do. The developer mind-set involves seeing the vision take on tangible structure, whether it means establishing task groups, responsibility/authority delegation, resource creation, time lines, job outlines, and any number of other details. These tend toward the managerial portion of the leadership process, but they must be overseen by the leader either directly or indirectly. Leaders who too quickly distance themselves from the vision project and/or move on to other tasks, will probably fail to see significant fruit from a vision.

For some people, just dreaming the dreams and getting them started is the sole satisfaction they desire. Unfortunately, they leave behind a number of disillusioned participants who are frustrated by the lack of commitment. The quantity and quality of those involved in the leadership process is a direct result of the degree a leader is involved in the development of a vision. If there are other significant leaders and people with influence who can run with a project, a leader can move on more quickly than when people must be recruited, trained, and held accountable personally by the leader. Every vision and organization is different, requiring the leader to respond individually to each situation.

Implementation involves committee work, group thinking, massaging the dream to make it fit the situation, and getting others involved. A person who pursues a vision alone is an entrepreneur, but not a leader. A wise leader will surround herself with people of appropriate gifts and skills who can complete the blueprints and begin the construction. A leader needs to have sufficient patience and teamwork abilities to gather together a group of people who will work together to fulfill the dream.

Characteristics of a Vision

A diamond is rated by characteristics such as its color, clarity, and weight/size. A vision is generally measured by three characteristics: intensity, clarity, and size. You can rate almost any vision on these three qualities.

Intensity: Intensity involves two elements. The first is how important the vision is, namely the impact it will make. The second element is the urgency of the dream. Peak intensity is when importance and urgency are both high, making the vision a present imperative.

How deeply do you feel the vision needs to happen? Never underestimate the power that is unleashed when a man or woman intensely believes in a cause. According to the oral tradition, a noted atheist, seen walking to a John Wesley revival meeting was asked, "I thought you didn't believe in God." The man responded, "I don't. But John Wesley sure does." This sort of passion is not solely a Christian virtue. Communism nearly overran the world because of the red-hot passion of its early leaders. The power for worldly objectives can be released by an enthusiastic leader who rallies followers to intensely pursue a single vision. If you catch on fire, people will come watch you burn. We have seen leaders with mediocre skills who were intensely zealous for a specific cause and who did incredible things.

What would you be willing to give up for this dream to happen? Every vision requires a sacrifice. That is part of the faith issue, the motivation issue. There are too many options available in life. Only those deemed most important will gain the attention of the crowd. A vision which requires no sacrifice ironically is not likely to move many people. People want to believe. They want to sink their lives into something. The most common problem in vision-fulfillment is a lack of intensity, such that no one is willing to pay the price to see the vision completed. For the caboose to get to the station, the engine has to go past the station. If you as a leader are not intensely committed to the vision, then more than likely others will not be. Exceptions arise when a follower catches a vision and develops an even more intense vision. However, this person usually becomes the leader. If the person does not have leadership qualities, then more than likely the vision will not go ahead.

Am I willing to die for this vision? Am I willing to sacrifice? These are the sort of issues at hand when discussing intensity. All visions need not be intense. We can only hitch our wagons to a few stars. There are many good causes available to us. The question is what cause am I going to buy in to? For what vision am I willing to sacrifice my time, money, and emotions? If a potential follower does not see a leader who intensely believes in a goal or project, it is doubtful that strong leadership will develop around this vision.

This passion is expressed in the scenario of a music student and teacher. "You just don't have it!" The music teacher is aggravated. The student has posture, fingering, notes all perfect; but his heart is not in it. Only his fingers are making a sort of music, but not the kind that will draw listeners to it. He has succeeded in boring even himself.

Urgency answers the questions: "When do we need to pursue this dream? Is time of the essence? Can we wait? Is this a fleeting opportunity, a critical moment, an emergency?" The must-do, have-to-do, gotta-pursue-it-right-away attitude is generally needed to make the vision a priority for would-be collaborators. With so many messages vying for attention these days, the only ones likely to capture the attention of a crowd are those presented as important and urgent.

Clarity: Clarity involves how clear the vision is in the mind of the leader. Is it in vivid color, black and white, or foggy? The greater the clarity, the better the chances for the vision to become reality. There is no better time to emerge as a leader than when a church or organization is in a fog; but to do this, the leader must have a clear description of where he is driving.

When the vision is at best hazy in the mind of the leader, the organization is likely to end up driving in circles. If you are leading a social cause such as Lincoln, Gandhi, or Martin Luther King, Jr., did, your vision is in terms of conditions and social order. If you are leading a building campaign, clarity in your vision may include the temporary convictions about wood, marble, and the decor of the new facility while emphasizing eternal ministry benefits. Most visions involve intangibles, and therefore require word pictures and redundancy to bring about clarification. A lack of clarity is a major reason why leaders are not more effective than they are. A lack of clarity in turn decreases intensity, because it is hard to hold on to a fog cloud.

Clarity helps bring people together. When a vision is only in outline form, there is a lot of room for vacillation and division. When a lot of people have a large number of opinions about the end result, it is not likely to unify the energies of a group synergistically. The game of basketball would be ruined if the metal rings were removed making scoring an obscure objective. Clarity increases the likelihood that there will be consistency among the people; and even though there are varying opinions, we are working together for a singular cause. A vision that is muddy tends to disperse its potential energy. People begin trying to fill in the pictures themselves, without a sense of what it should look like. Just as the sun shining through a magnifying glass can produce intense heat, a vision that is focused empowers leadership far more than one that is only half-baked. Clarity is improved with redundancy, variety of approaches, and suitable feedback opportunities. Models, visual aids, and tangible media where appropriate can help. One of the best ways to measure clarity is to ask other leaders and nonleaders to say what they are hearing. This sort of feedback helps the leader know what needs to be said, to whom and to what degree. Various individuals and groups will perceive the vision differently. Visions rarely bake evenly.

Clarity alone does not guarantee leadership effectiveness. Often a leader has a very specific idea of what should happen, but the problem is that no one else sees it that way. This results in an imitation of Don Quixote challenging the windmills. Although inspiring, it is not necessarily fruitful. The best vision begins in the mind and soul of the leader and then gets molded and becomes incarnate by the people.

Size: People are rarely moved by visions that require no more faith or courage than is commonly being expressed. Minute missions do not spark the interest of those who long for meaning, purpose, and significance. The power of a vision is most often found in its shear breadth and depth. Someone said that people do not follow plans, they follow leaders. I understand the rationale, but there comes a point in the birth of a vision when that the vision soon takes on a personality of its own. If the vision is clear enough and large enough, it will inspire the following of people more than any single leader. This is the key that allows leaders to come and go, and churches, ministries, and organizations to continue. God uses men and women to raise up new dreams; but once raised, these dreams become the sort of things that attract people. Size is a big part of this issue.

The concern of every human is going to the grave without a sense of significance. You want to think "I made a difference with my life." By aligning with projects that are bigger than yourself you can fulfill your need for destiny and purpose. Robert Schuller admits that it was easier to raise millions for a Crystal Cathedral than it was to get a few hundred dollars for a church dishwasher. Why? Because people long to be inspired by something big, something that transcends their own little world. Together, there is great power. Together, great matters can be accomplished. The world is constantly seeking those with the will and the ability to gather us together in groups such that the outcome of our corporate efforts is far greater than the sum total of our individual energies. This is the miracle of leadership.

Do not waste your time with minuscule missions. They do not have the power to turn heads, let alone souls. As leaders, we are in the soul business, stretching people to trust God with their time, money, and emotions. We are called to push people over the edge of faith and to realize that God is in us to do, not just to be. God never called anyone to a task that did not produce a certain amount of fear and also require risk. When the angel unleashed the call to Mary, Joseph, and the shepherds, the first words uttered were, "Fear not." When God met Moses in the burning bush, and throughout the Old and New Testaments, he was constantly calling his people to get beyond themselves. The size of a vision is crucial to the effectiveness of its completion.

Naturally, size alone is not the key, for pie-in-the-sky dreamers come and go throughout history. Many more fail than succeed. Some pastors say that their church is going to be a 3,000 or a 10,000 member church. It is possible. Although tagging a number, square footage, or logarithmic growth pattern on your organization is not the content of the vision, this kind of specificity can engage interest in a vision. People want to make a difference, and the size of a vision addresses this desire.

A leader's chief responsibility is to make certain there is a clear vision for the leadership group. This vision becomes the rallying point, the shared dream, the basis from which goals and objectives are formulated. It is the inspirational paste that glues the team together and helps new people catch fire. The ability to initiate, cast, and implement vision is perhaps the most important single skill of anyone who would lead. Without this vital element, the most gifted leader is rendered powerless. It is admittedly simplistic to reduce leading to any given aspect of a very complicated process, but if you plan to take only one learning from this book I would advise you to spend your time and energy producing a vision.

CHAPTER 11

THE POWER OF MOMENTUM

Understanding the Power of Momentum

One of the most important and least discussed elements of any leadership equation is the concept of momentum. The "big mo," as many refer to it, can make or break an individual in terms of leading ability and thus determine the success or failure of an endeavor.

Leadership is much like a recipe. For a chocolate cake you need ingredients such as flour, milk, eggs, baking soda, sugar, and so forth. You can get everything nearly right, but when the cake comes out of the oven it can be delicious or lousy depending on minute ingredient differences and baking conditions. The outcome is a chemical reaction. The great chefs know the secrets that turn seemingly ordinary recipes into masterpieces. Anyone who analyzes successful leaders and their endeavors understand that outward appearances such as the quality of the services, talents, and facilities may not add up to a successful scenario. Still, the results cannot be denied, and the people keep coming back for more in increasing numbers.

The reason it is so difficult to replicate the success in copycat situations is the unsung element of momentum. Momentum is often like the magical pixie dust that transforms ordinary people into superheroes and otherwise mundane events and activities into divine phenomena. When momentum kicks in to a church or program, the synergistic effect is contagious. Because humans are social beings, they look to one an other for cues. When an item such as a clothing label, a song, a type of dance, a singer, actor, or theme becomes popular, fads seemingly spread overnight. When this sort of activity takes place within an organization, leadership appears destined for effectiveness.

As in physics, an organization at rest tends to remain at rest and an organization in motion tends to remain in motion. It is easier to keep the momentum in an organization going when momentum is present. A related law warns us that it requires more energy to initially move a body at rest than it does to keep a moving body going. An effective leader recognizes that it will require significant focus and effort to develop the momentum the church needs, much like a rocket requires more thrust at liftoff than when it is orbiting the earth. Organizational gravity keeps it from moving freely.

An effective leader understands the characteristics of negative and positive momentum. This enables the leader to identify why some organizations seem so strong and why other groups are so difficult to move.

Characteristics of High Momentum

Leaders are perceived to be better than they really are. Have you ever heard another person rave about a certain leader, who seemed merely above average to your critical eye? Momentum can make average people seem special and above average people appear phenomenal. Great leaders are often just good leaders who by luck, shrewd engineering, or divine appointment were able to realize a certain level of momentum in their organization. Suddenly, people begin quoting them; trying to emulate and model them; and seeking them to author books, endorse products, and promote special events. Very often the main thing that changes is perception. People do not respond to reality. They respond to their perceptions of reality. Perception is social reality, and positive momentum tends to change our perceptions positively about leaders.

Products and organizations are perceived to be better than they really are. Just as people associated with winning teams rise in value, so do the products and the reputation of the organization. High momentum provides that winning feeling that elevates the perceived value of things associated with the high MO team.

Negativity fades into the background. High MO churches appear to have very few negative people. They may exist, but they receive little air time. When momentum is high, people tend to celebrate and focus on the good. Naysayers are a minority and rarely get attention because people are busy focusing on what is happening well.

Major objectives become the emphasis. High MO churches major on majors and minor on minors. A group with vision tends to be busy with what is important versus trivial pursuit. The idea of being about what is important, focusing on what makes a difference, and keeping the big picture in mind is prevalent. This focus on priorities in turn perpetuates the probability of effectiveness.

Enthusiasm tends to add fuel and feed the momentum even more. Nothing succeeds like success. People want to be associated with a winning team; so when spirit is high, growth is happening, and God seems to be blessing your church, chances are good that the momentum will continue or increase.

Characteristics of Low/No Momentum

The leader is perceived to be worse than he really is. When momentum is at low ebb, the same person who may have seized the peak prior can become an outcast. It was only a few days from the time Jesus rode into Jerusalem on palm branches to the time he was crucified. Winston Churchill was Britain's favorite during World War II, but the loss of wartime enthusiasm resulted in his inability to be reelected. Leaders are often perceived as smaller than they really are in negative momentum. Others will not seriously consider their opinions, respect their leading, or respond to their ideas or requests. The only difference in being deemed a loser versus a winner is often perception due to a lack of momentum.

Products and organization are perceived to be worse than they really may be. When things are not progressing well, we tend to develop negative images of programs and the church itself. A program in a low momentum church will be valued far less than the identical program in a high momentum church, because of its context, association, and perception.

Negative people and comments emerge and vie for attention. Negative attitude cycles are easy to develop when momentum is low. We tend to see what is wrong and what needs to be changed, because we are not preoccupied with the excitement of what is going well. Realize that this negativity is not necessarily a fair expression of the state of the church, but that your church is probably suffering from negative momentum. A reactionary person will strive to address the negativity. A proactive leader will attempt to build a bonfire of excitement in order to outshine the naysayers.

Trivia and pettiness become favorite pastimes. In addition to the negativity which arises in low momentum churches, an emphasis on minor issues becomes the predominant theme. I have listened in meetings where people began micromanaging what they thought was wrong with a certain service or ministry. Fixing the minutiae was not the solution. Building momentum and focusing on bigger issues was. When people lack vision, they begin swatting gnats.

There is difficulty in attracting quality people even when individual products or events may appear to be good. The inherent problem with negative momentum is that the cycle is hard to interrupt. Momentum is nearly always increased in a church with growing numbers, but new people are not likely to come to an organization lacking momentum. Most pastors have had the experience of watching new people attend when things were less than exciting, only to never see them again.

Dealing with Momentum

Momentum is both strong and brittle. Cast iron can be very strong and yet can easily crack. That seems like a paradox, but it helps as a physical analogy of momentum. When momentum is strong, a person can do almost anything to the organization itself and it will not feel the effect. Momentum to an organization is like adrenalin to the human body. When adrenalin is surging into the human system, it can run longer, stronger, and is far less prone to feel pain than when adrenalin is not present. Great strength and resiliency exist when momentum is strong. I am often amused when I attend church growth seminars and hear pastors explaining what they did to "make their church grow." I appreciate what they are saying and believe in part that some of the things they "did" brought about the initial inertia. However, what most of these wonderful people are overlooking is that once momentum begins, it often does not matter what program was or was not begun. In essence, the program or plan may have only appeared productive because it received its blessing from the momentum.

A leader experiencing momentum can often just let the surge of energy carry him along, much like a surfer rides a wave. Momentum has the ability to make heroes out of otherwise quite ordinary people. If the wave of momentum lasts long enough, institutions and small empires can result. The leader becomes a living legend and tribal stories told of this person take on cultlike popularity. The aura of such a person allows for more and more subsequent successes to be generated, such that momentum has within itself the ability to regenerate itself.

Although someone says that success came via a bus ministry, a seeker sensitive service, an evangelism explosion thrust, or special worship, it may or may not have been the catalyzing force. Momentum often plays tricks on us in understanding why things "happen." This is what is commonly referred to as superstitious behavior. For example, when a baseball player hits a homerun and discovers that he wore his socks inside out that day, he will probably wear his socks inside out the next few games to see if it changes his luck. In similar fashion, we assume that whatever we were doing prior to a surge in momentum is the primary catalyst for it. Therefore, we package it and try to market it as the key for others to use, claiming that you cannot deny the results. Just because a phenomenon happens with something else does not mean it causes it.

Momentum is at times brittle in that a single event or decision can bring the quick demise to an otherwise resilient group. For example, if a strong leader has a moral failure or if a scandal breaks out at the right time, the burgeoning spirit of euphoria can quickly change to a sense of loss and failure. Often when this happens, there is a strong response of anger as people feel betrayed that this person would take from them their sense of success. The surge of euphoria during high momentum creates so much hope and goodwill in people that the person who helped induce this condition may transition from hero to traitor when failure occurs. The history books are full of companies, nations, and ministries that suddenly came to a screeching halt because of an internal scandal or leader demise during the height of momentum. Like a strong football player with a trick knee, the organization with momentum that appeared unstoppable can suddenly halt midstream.

Leaders need to get out of the way of momentum and let it run its course within reason. The most alive and dynamic organizations often appear to be a bit chaotic. They seem to thrive on chaos. There is so much happening that no one can control it, and this often allows the momentum to continue.

Leaders can ruin the momentum by trying to get control. Long-term examples of this are denominations that began as revivals spawned by the Holy Spirit under a certain leader's ministry. Eventually, infrastructure was created to better organize the success to the point that eventually the organization stalled and lost the energy of the original momentum. This happens time after time, such that God has to let some movements die and create others. Old wineskins do not allow for much elasticity, so new wineskins are needed for expansion. Giving birth is easier than raising the dead. What appears to be transformational and revolutionary eventually becomes traditional and even bureaucratic. Every organization and church has its life span. It is usually difficult for major new momentum to take place in an old organization without significant change and restructuring. Luther's desire to bring change to the Catholic church resulted in the Protestant movement, and Wesley's desire to change the Anglican Church produced a new denomination.

The best thing for leaders to do is to get out of momentum's way and see how they may be impeding the movement of the Spirit and/or the progress. Certain people will emerge whose earnest interests slow momentum's gain. This is not to suggest that a leader adopt an irresponsible position of doing nothing. Certain structure, staffing, and resource allotment can liberate momentum. Some people feel uncomfortable when things appear to be getting out of hand and growth does not seem manageable. Fear can kill momentum. Leaders by nature are able to feel somewhat comfortable with ambiguity. The discerning leader will capitalize on momentum and allow for a little reckless enjoyment of letting things happen naturally instead of trying to manage the church for better control. Control will often kill momentum, much like a parent who tells his celebrating child to "sit still and behave yourself." Momentum is an organization's way of celebrating its life and health.

Leaders must be sensitive in order to channel the momentum. Momentum can get out of hand. While living in southern California, I have seen what fires can do to the landscape. Occasionally, a controlled fire will be intentionally set in order to cut down on the risk of natural fire. But if the winds pick up the flames, they can get out of control so that the fire set to help results in terrible damage. History is full of examples of movements gone awry due to their own success. Leaders can get carried away with the success, take credit for the effectiveness, and develop cultlike characteristics. Unbridled energy can draw people who are power-possessive but who do not have the character and integrity needed to handle such authority, thus undermining the ultimate objectives. Momentum can draw many spectators who never fully commit to the organization, and who just as easily leave when the momentum plateaus or declines.

So many people talk about handling failure, but few discuss the effective management of success. Is bigger better? Is more best? Downsizing in business has brought in the idea that success may be more a matter of quality than quantity. No one is denying that God can and wants to do some big things, but even Christian leaders must recognize the potential danger that lies in momentum that gets out of hand. That is why the element of incarnational leadership and true dependence on God are so important when momentum comes into a church or ministry.

When momentum is in, take advantage of it. Effective organizations have crests and troughs, just like ocean waves. Some Sundays and some weeks, it seems that nothing can go wrong. At other seasons, nothing seems to go right. This is the magical, mystical, chemical side of leadership. It eludes the most analytical detective and avoids the grasp of the finest church growth consultants. No one can explain it. But the wise leader understands that when momentum is coming in and is at high tide, he needs to do whatever he can to seize the moment. This is like paying the bills when the money is in the bank, because there is a good chance that it will not always be there. Harness this energy to make changes, start new programs, and get things going that cannot get done when momentum is at low ebb.

The temptation is to sit back and enjoy momentum's presence and let up on leading during these times. We work so hard during the low momentum times, feeling parched and depleted, that we long to just stop and soak up the showers of blessings when momentum returns. Joseph advised Pharaoh to build storehouses during the seven years of feast in order to prepare for the seven years of famine. A good leader will strive to use the energy from the momentum to recruit new people, set new objectives, and enhance programs and resources where possible so that if and when the momentum decreases, the church will be better off for it and less likely to sink back to its previous position. Enjoy the experience, but enjoy it while you are quickly preparing reservoirs for less blessed days.

When momentum is short term and when it is not fully utilized, a church can be worse off for it. Like a dieter who loses weight temporarily only to gain it all back plus some, an organization that experiences limited momentum can be set back because of this short spurt of excitement and growth. People can become disillusioned by the temporary sense of euphoria and hope and cannot bounce back when it is diminished. A leader strives to use momentum much like a person climbs a rope. The person pulls his body up the rope and then quickly changes hand positions, placing each hand higher on the rope, then using the higher position to pull up his body one more time. When he rests, he is farther up than previously. The leader who strives to milk the momentum will help the organization inch forward so that if and when the momentum goes out, it is in a better position than before. This better position will thus allow the church to be more effective because of the momentum and not worse off for it.

Do whatever it takes (within reason), to build momentum in your organization. "Inch by inch anything's a cinch" is a great slogan on perseverance. More often than not, leaders who appear to be overnight successes have been sowing their seed through small, well performed tasks. Scripture says that if we are obedient in the small things, God will put us in charge of larger things. The leader experiencing momentum has often paid his dues by way of less exciting times. The point of this principle has to do with doing whatever is necessary to help induce momentum when it is not present in an organization, because momentum will tend to take care of itself. You can only achieve some things with momentum.

I have seen it happen time after time that good leaders get discouraged when they do all the right things but still do not see the fruit of momentum. This is a tough lot to bear. I do not have any answers except to advise them to keep utilizing all the resources, ideas, and opportunities that arise. Sometimes it is just a matter of timing. Sometimes it is doing the same thing over and over again, so that it finally takes off. The danger is to quit. Sometimes the dream has to die before God resurrects it. God has often gotten people to a place of breaking, a stage of impotency, prior to his blessing (for example, Abraham and Sarah, Zechariah and Elizabeth). Giving up is not the same as quitting. When you quit, you need to leave the organization and go somewhere else. When you give up, you basically admit you have done all you can, and there is nothing humanly possible left to do as a leader.

Sometimes God acknowledges this state of surrender and then brings momentum and blessing to a mission or ministry. Sometimes he does not. It is the leader's task, as long as he is the leader of the church or organization, to do whatever is in his realms of creativity and resourcefulness to make things happen. He is to be the initiator of what would produce momentum. Like Sherlock Holmes, he must investigate every person or situation that is impeding momentum. Sometimes he is the problem. Healthy organizations grow naturally. Our job as leaders is to help cure the illnesses and remove the blockages. Obviously, this is an "us" job. We cannot do it alone. We need to listen well, read well, and seek others' views.

Generally, a leader should not quit until he has tried everything he deems possible to bring about healthy organizational change. Too many people quit too soon because of discouragement, lack of perseverance, and fear. If a leader has tried everything within his strength to initiate momentum and change and has nothing left to give, then moving should be a strong recommendation. If this pattern persists over the course of several years in various locations, the leader may need to consider some other vocation than leading. Again, the call to minister is not necessarily the same as the call to lead. A nonleader needs to seek out ministry roles where leading is not required for effectiveness, as in many staff and academic roles or where church polity does not expect the pastor to lead.

Because his primary responsibility is for organizational health, the pastor must honestly face the possibility that he is keeping the organization from being what it needs to be. A leader with integrity will admit this and move on. Too many would-be leaders hang on too long and avoid the inevitable decision that they cannot bring about organizational momentum and that they should move on to let someone else give it a try. Happy is the organization who has a leader who knows when it is time to move.

Closing Thoughts

The new church paradigm is upon us and seeks pastors who would primarily serve as leaders. There will undoubtedly be positions and opportunities for those called to serve as hands-on ministers and church managers. Do not be discouraged if you recognize few leader abilities in yourself. Your role in the Body of Christ is just as important. If you lack such resources, serve to the best of your ability in other capacities, but realize how leadership works and what needs to happen in your church for positive change. If you do see leader abilities in yourself, charge forward. The times have never called for more and better leaders than today. God is raising up a new type of pastor who would lead his church during these times of change. He is looking specifically for pastors who lead with passion, with the mind of a priest and the soul of a prophet.

NOTES

1. Retool or Retire

1. George Barna, *Today's Pastors* (Ventura, Calif.: Regal, 1993), p. 117.
2. Ibid., p. 122.

5. Incarnational Leadership

1. A large portion of this chapter is a revision of the Epilogue in *Broken in the Right Place*, by Alan E. Nelson (Nashville: Thomas Nelson, 1994).
2. *In the Name of Jesus* by Henri Nouwen (New York: Crossroad, 1990), p. 57.
3. *Servant Leadership*, by Robert Greenleaf (New York: Paulist Press, 1977).

6. Leading the Way Versus Holding the Fort

1. Abraham Zaleznick, "Managers and Leaders: Are They Different?" (*Harvard Business Review*, May-June, 1977), p. 69.
2. M. E. Trammel and H. Reynolds, *Executive Leadership* (Englewood Cliffs, N.J.: Prentice Hall, 1981), pp. 33-35.
3. Zaleznick, "Managers and Leaders" p. 72.
4. Ibid., p. 73.
5. Ibid., pp. 74-75.

253
N424
C.1

91128

LINCOLN CHRISTIAN COLLEGE AND SEMINARY

3 4711 00092 0894